Notre Dame Football

THE T FORMATION

Notre Dame Football

THE T FORMATION

Frank Leahy

NEW YORK

PRENTICE-HALL, INC

PRENTICE-HALL BOOKS ON HEALTH AND SPORTS
Edited by Elmer D. Mitchell

To

the memory of

Coach Knute K. Rockne

Preface

THIS HUMBLE EFFORT is dedicated to the fine gentlemen, past and present, who have made our profession such a well-regarded occupation in the scheme of things that is known as the American way of life. Its contents and the work that went into the preparation of same are dedicated to the coaches of America in general, but particularly to the greatest coach that the game of football has ever known, the late Knute Rockne.

In dedicating this book to the men who have made a life's work out of building boys on the athletic field rather than in the classroom, it is our deep-seated conviction that the tribute is being offered to as excellent a group of individuals as this nation knows in any of its professions. Admitting considerable bias in such a judgment, my feelings along these lines have been supported by the opinion of some great military leaders of our land.

During the course of World War II there was endless evidence of the part that the coaches of this country played in building better manhood through competitive athletics. I can think of instances, far too numerous to mention, of young lads whose performances in the armed forces reflected credit not only upon themselves but upon the coaches who had taught them, on the athletic fields of our great country, lessons that paid dividends to our side in the greatest victory of our times.

The performances of our coaches have paid off, too, in the peacetime life of these United States; and I feel it a real privilege to be one of a group that has won for itself a position of respect in every community, large and small, from coast to coast.

For our fellow coaches, then, we write this preface, with the expressed hope that their influence for good may continue long after all of us have named our last starting lineup.

FRANK LEAHY

Table of Contents

List of Photographs

(between pages 132 and 133)

Notre Dame Football

THE T FORMATION

Introduction

~~~~~~

1

Get to Know Your Players

SINCE ENTERING the coaching profession nineteen years ago we have always believed that in order to achieve the best player-coach relations it is absolutely necessary that the head coach meet with his candidates on the opening day of practice for the express purpose of outlining, completely, what he will expect from each and every aspirant during the entire season. If such a plan is formulated definitely on the initial day, there should be no basis for differences of opinion throughout the year.

The medium we have used to put across these ideas to our football players is what we have entitled a "Get Acquainted Talk." Such an informal chat familiarizes our lads with our simple requests, and lets them know what the policies will be for all the practice sessions as well as the games.

BASIC REQUIREMENTS

We tell all of our men that the first and foremost requisite of a good football player is that he must have a *burning desire* to play the game. There is absolutely no substitute for this. In the history of football we have had all kinds of men who have become stars—big men, small men, fast men, and slow men, but we have never seen a man achieve gridiron greatness who did not possess a burning desire to win. If you look into the past, you will find that all successful teams which won many games in the fourth quarter possessed this desire, to a man. This is one requisite that must be inherent in a player. It can be stimulated by means of pep talks or existing conditions, but it first must be in the lad. We instruct our boys to think always in terms of winning games. People who want to win stand a very good chance of doing just that.

The second requirement in a football candidate is one that takes precedence, at Notre Dame, over desire; that is, to maintain a high scholastic average. At our University it is necessary for all students to maintain an over-all average of 70 percent in order to pass. Yet in order for a student to participate in intercollegiate athletics, he must obtain a qualitative average of 77 percent. Although at times this rule seems hard on the athletes, it is really a great thing for them. It makes them work that much harder to achieve success. The University authorities feel that if a man is going to leave Notre Dame with a reputation as an athlete, then he also will leave with an academic record that will reflect credit on his Alma Mater. Many of our football aspirants have to get up early every morning in order to keep up in their classwork; however, they make themselves do it, and when they graduate they are thankful for the hard-earned degree that they receive.

The next trait for which we look is aggressiveness. This is an asset that can be developed in an athlete, although naturally it is more prevalent in some than in others. An aggressive team is always a dangerous team. We try to train our lads to be exceptionally aggressive at the time of a pass interception. In our opinion, one of the signs of a truly great team is the ability to switch immediately from defense to offense, and to start blocking instead of tackling.

We have found that if an athlete is willing to pay the price for success he will receive his share of it. It is necessary for many football players to punish themselves severely in order to get into top physical condition.   Those who are willing to work at this continually will soon find that they are rapidly moving past boys of equal ability who are wont to take the easy road.   Every member of our football squad is fully cognizant of the fact that there is no stationary period in football. Either a player improves somewhat each day, or he deteriorates.   We ask our lads to strive diligently for perfection during every practice session.   If a boy will improve himself one percent during individual drills, he will find that toward the end of the season he is quite capable of performing the tasks that are asked of him.

A little drill that we like to have our boys perform consists of looking into the mirror occasionally and evaluating themselves.   Just let them look at themselves and concentrate on how well they are doing as compared to how well they can do. The boys who work the hardest will find that they gain incentive by these little meetings with themselves, whereas the loafers will either take themselves to task, or will fall by the wayside.   Let each and every boy ask himself if he is giving 100 percent for his teammates and his school.

To have a successful football season, it is imperative that you have a group of young men who are willing to make sacrifices.   First in this line is that the entire squad must help themselves to get into good physical condition by abstaining from all tobacco and alcoholic beverages.   Since no one knows exactly how far an athlete can carry these habits before they become injurious to his physical condition, we ask our players to abstain 100 percent during the training periods. As well as being good physically, such abstention is good for the character because it builds will power in the young men. Also, it is a good example for the youngsters of America who idolize the athletes in all parts of our country.

You get what you give, and very little more.   We always tell our players about the farmer who for many years had been trading his butter to a grocery store for various necessities. After twenty years, the storekeeper accused the farmer of bringing in only seven-eighths of a pound of butter each week. The farmer was hurt and answered that he had a homemade scale, on which, each Saturday morning, he would balance his butter with a pound of flour that he had received from the grocery store. Although this story lacks humor, it gets our point across to our squad members. We find that invariably the eleven men who start for Notre Dame on Saturday are eleven of the hardest workers—men who are willing to pay the price for success and subsequent renown.

We have no room on our squad for a man who gives up easily. We of the coaching staff do not claim to be infallible, and many times a worthy lad may escape us for a short while, but if the boy will not give up, and if he keeps working day-by-day, he will soon achieve the recognition that is rightfully his. A concrete example of this fact is Coy McGee, a 141-pound halfback, who recently performed admirably on the gridiron for Notre Dame during three years. Before the war Coy was unable to make the grade at another school because he was too small. After his discharge from the service, this un-renowned youth enrolled at Notre Dame, and came out for football. About midway through the 1946 season we began to notice this little halfback who was giving the varsity so much difficulty when they scrimmaged the "B" squad. Once given a chance to run with the "A" team, Coy never relinquished the gain. By the end of the season he was pretty much of a fixture in our backfield, making runs of seventy and forty-four yards to score two touchdowns in the season's finale against the University of Southern California.

If an individual does not think in terms of team success, then he is of no use to you, the coach. Any time we spot signs of selfishness in a lad we have an immediate chat with him. If he does not get such ideas out of his mind, we demand that he turn in his suit. Many times in a crucial moment the entire outcome of the game will depend upon a team unity that will result in a great effort toward the end that just one man get across the goal line. If the quarterback calls on the left halfback to carry the mail into pay territory, the other two backs must block and fake just as hard as they would have run had their number been called. We are exceptionally proud of the feeling that exists among our Notre Dame players in this regard: each man is genuinely happy to see the ball go into the opponent's end zone, regardless of whose arm it is in.

Going hand in hand with the requirement of team unity is loyalty to school, to coaches, and to teammates. A thought that often comes to us is, "Where else will the young men of America learn loyalty if they don't learn it on the athletic field?"

A daily check with the assistant coaches is another suggestion that we make to our boys. Have them ask what they did incorrectly on the day before, and from then on they should concentrate diligently on their weaknesses. Players should never be afraid to ask what is wrong or how to correct it. We ask them not to waste time with maneuvers that come easily. Every available minute should be spent on things that are difficult to perform. A player who works daily on his weaknesses will find that he does not have nearly as many at the close of the season.

PRACTICE

Be prompt. Inform your players at the start of the season how long your practice sessions will be. Tell them what time you want them on the field, and what time you will dismiss them. We have a student manager check in the squad members each day, and all those who report on time are finished exactly two hours after the practice period commences. I like to have our assistant coaches on the field fifteen minutes prior to the beginning of practice. This will give them ample time to answer any questions that their respective players may care to ask.

We have found that a two-hour session brings the best results. When the practice runs any longer, we have noticed men holding back in order that they may show a strong finish. A man in top condition can practice for two hours and turn in the type of work we desire of our aspirants. You should start work immediately at the time prescribed. Have each man trot out onto the field. No lagging along should be permitted.

Prior to starting the actual practice we ask our players to do three simple things, under the direction of a member of the coaching staff:

1st. The seat roll, which consists of sitting on the ground and moving the body in a rotary motion from the hips.

2nd. The lineman's charge, in which the men assume a lineman's stance; next they lunge forward, extending their body completely, and then return to position.

3rd. The hurdler's spread. The title is self-explanatory since the boys spread their legs out on the ground as if they were about to go over a hurdle. From this position they reach out with both hands, touching first the front foot and then the rear.

All three exercises should take a period of about fifteen minutes before the "All Up" is sounded. Upon hearing this call, all the men should run immediately to join the group where their assistant coach is stationed.

Group work is the medium through which all of our men learn their fundamentals. We have our linemen work against their assistant coach daily. In these sessions the coach gives his men the benefit of his experience in a very practical way. It is mandatory that our linemen do their best against an assistant because he does his very best to show them how an opponent *could* make them look very bad on a Saturday afternoon. Our men are told many times that the assistants are trying, not to show them up, but rather to keep them from being shown up at some future date. It is in these drills that the men develop much of their finesse. Such simple maneuvers as the head fake and the forearm shiver are perfected in these brief sessions. Next, the coaches will have the lads work against each other so that they may see how they shape up against men fairly commensurate in ability. This is where we find out who the real battlers are. It is too late on Saturday afternoon to get this information. Make sure that each movement is done with a maximum amount of hustle. Instill this habit in practice and it will always be prevalent at game time. Take time to explain thoroughly why you have these drills, since this will avoid the possibility of anyone having hard feelings toward the assistant coaches.

While the above activity is going on among the linemen we have our backs work out in individual groups. Four backs and one center comprise each group. Have them run plays up and down the field for about ten minutes. This will loosen them up in regard to handling the ball, as well as aiding them in the perfection of their timing on the various plays.

The greatest player in the world cannot help out if he does not know his assignments. We have a contest during spring practice each year to see who has kept the best notebook throughout the training period. Each player should study his plays frequently. He should know what move he must make on every play and also what his teammates are doing, so that he will not hinder their progress in any way. This is especially important on pass plays. Our thinking on this is that if a decoy does not know what the intended receiver is going to do, he will not make a very good decoy. Make your study of plays interesting and the boys will enjoy learning them. We have an assistant coach stand before our group, flash the various plays on large cards, and ask the players to call them out by name.

We ask all of our squad members who are sitting on the bench during a game to stand up after each score, regardless of which team scores. Let the men on the field know that the entire squad is behind them 100 percent. Never allow any shouting at the officials. Such conduct reflects very badly on the school, the coach, and the players. Also, if the game is close in the fourth quarter and the official is stumped as to which way to call a decision, his sixth sense may react in favor of the players who have conducted themselves as gentlemen throughout the contest.

When a player comes off the field, have him greeted by a man who plays the same position, and let him talk over the situation with his prospective substitute. We are not in favor of the coach spending his time with the players when there is so much going on in front of him. Try to develop friendships among aspirants for the same positions. Have them striving diligently for the first team, yet willing to tip the others off as to their shortcomings. Two of our right ends during the 1946-47-48 seasons, Bill Wightkin and Leon Hart, were roommates and close friends off the field and outstanding performers on the gridiron.

Every member of our squad is required to call each of the assistants, "Coach." We tell the boys that we do not care how they address the head coach, but the above mentioned degree of respect must be shown to the assistants. In our opinion, it is necessary to establish a teacher-pupil relationship between both parties. We would never expect to see a student enter a classroom and call his professor by his first name, and we feel that the same should hold true on the football field. I always refer to the assistants by this title and insist that the boys do likewise.

We inform our candidates that criticism is like money; they

should not worry about it, but they should worry over the lack of it. Not one member of our staff ever criticizes a lad because of any enjoyment he gets out of the job; he does so because he sees the boy making a mistake and wants to help him correct it. The boy who is never criticized is the one who should worry. In all probability this lad is doing so many things wrong that the coaches do not know just where to start with their constructive criticism. The men that we criticize are the ones we are planning to have help us out during the fall.

We like a boy who will look his coach right in the eye when he is talking to him. If a boy comes up to me and starts talking while he is looking at the ground, I begin to wonder if he isn't hiding something from me. We ask all of our men to step right up, address us clearly, and look directly at us during the entire conversation. This is a good habit for a boy to acquire and carry through life.

"DON'TS"

This completes the "musts" that we specify for our players during their days at Notre Dame; however, before we go onto the practice field we also give a list of "don'ts," which in our mind are equally important and must be adhered to if the boy intends to remain on our squad.

The number one "don't" refers to the use of profanity. We do not have it among our coaches and we will not allow it among our players. This outward sign of an anemic vocabulary is something that can be curbed in young men, and this should be done before they are allowed to go out into the world as representatives of the school at which you are privileged to coach.

Sitting down is a habit that is never exercised on the Notre Dame practice field. Boys get lazy if they are seated. Plan your practice sessions so that they will have something to keep them busy for the two hours they are on the field.

Punching by any member of our group is not tolerated. It is the sign of a coward, and if our men cannot win games without having to resort to these illegal tactics, then we request that they obtain their college education at some other institution. Many times the easy way to rid yourself of a very determined opponent is to punch him, but the man who employs this method is the type of man who will quit when the going gets real tough, and you will wish that you had gotten rid of him at an earlier date.

Alibis do not interest our coaching staff. We usually have a fairly good idea of why a ball carrier does not score or why a tackler misses his man, and we do not care to hear the blame placed on another person. As mentioned before, no one on the entire staff misses very many operations on the field; thus, the "alibier" is likely to find his story contradicted by someone who saw the true situation.

Gambling is "taboo" among Notre Dame football players. There is no doubt that it helps pass the time on long trips, but there is the ever-present danger of solid friendships being broken up over the loss of money. This, like many other habits, has no definite point beyond which one can say indulgence is bad; therefore, we do not allow it to be carried on at all by our squad members.

Egotism can be very dangerous to a successful football team. Coach Rockne used to define egotism as an anesthetic which deadens the pain of stupidity. Our best results have been obtained by treating every member of our squad in the same way, regardless of his relative ability. I can truthfully state, without fear of contradiction from anyone, that in my years as Head Coach of Football at Notre Dame we have never been troubled with the slightest sign of egotism on our squad. However, if it is not present, don't relax—keep a constant guard out against it.

We ask our players not to leave their character on the football field; they should always display that which makes them successful athletes. Many people know a school only through the players that represent it. We ask our players to act like gentlemen at all times, and we require that they wear a coat and tie into dining cars and restaurants while representing the University on a trip. Such things may seem very small, but they leave a strong impression on people who come in contact with our varsity off the field. We also stress the proper method of meeting people. The lads should shake their hand firmly and inform them that they are glad to meet them.

The manner of speech of traveling football players should be representative of college men. Young boys are quick to pick up words and phrases they have heard athletes use, and this can be either very good or very bad. Ask the boys not to do anything that will not reflect well on the school. Victory means nothing unless you can truthfully say that you are champions off the field as well as on it.

It is quite true that most of this "Get Acquainted Talk" is very elementary, but we have found it invaluable in indoctrinating our lads in our methods of doing business. What each and every coach must realize is that we are all in a wonderful position to raise the prestige of the coaching profession. Strive diligently to assure that every athlete will go out into the world equipped to show that he has derived many benefits from his training periods. If the business and professional world becomes permeated with outstanding gentlemen who have been outstanding athletes, the men in those professions will begin to see what a superb job the coaches of America are doing with the youth of the country.

2

The Notre Dame "T" Formation

THE PURPOSE OF this book is not to try to prove that the Notre Dame "T" is the best in the country, but rather to give to our readers the same material that we give to our players. This information is the best that we of the coaching staff have to offer, and we like to feel that it will measure up to the majority of offenses in the football world today.

We thought over the situation for a long time before definitely deciding to install the "T" at our Alma Mater. Some people went so far as to say that in so doing we were disrespectful to the greatest coach of them all, Knute Rockne. I am inclined to feel otherwise, having had the privilege of playing under Coach Rockne, and I believe, in all sincerity, that if he were living today Coach Rockne would have been one of the first men to install the "T" formation in college football. After conducting a thorough study of this fast-striking formation, we made a list of all the advantages of the "T." These we compared to the advantages of the old Notre Dame system, and decided it would be a wise move on our part to change our offensive set-up. I am very happy to say that the authorities here at Notre Dame were most agreeable to the planned renovation. We should like to devote the next few pages to an outline of the aforementioned advantages of our plan of attack.

ADVANTAGES OF THE "T" FORMATION

To my thinking, the greatest advantage of the "T" is that your center becomes 100 percent a blocker.   He actually is into the play before any other lineman because he knows exactly when the ball is going to be snapped, and he starts to operate accordingly.   The "T" center gives no tip-off to the opponent, since he does not have to look through his legs to see where his target is.   He can feel him.

The plays strike much more swiftly in the "T," thus allowing the coach to use the element of surprise more effectively. The fact that the quarterback is partially covered by the center permits greater deception.   Although there is but one basic formation, a maximum number of variations can be formulated without trouble to anyone except the opponent. Such movements as sending a flanker, or man-in-motion, or spreading the ends are very disconcerting to the enemy. When the man goes in motion the opposition must send a man out to guard him.   This automatically gets the defender out of the play.   The flanker who goes wide can never be held in on a pass play, and he has many chores to perform.   He may be a pass receiver, a decoy, a blocker, or a lateral receiver. Most important, he is always a reconnaissance man, and he should report to the quarterback as soon as he returns to the huddle.   Perhaps he is not being well guarded when he goes out in the flat, or perhaps two men are moving with him and leaving a spot for an end to catch a short pass.

The backs arrive at the holes exactly when the linemen initiate the contact.   Since this is true, it is not required that the holes remain open for long.   Thus we can employ man-for-man blocking and allow the linemen on the opposite side of the line from the hole to release their blocks and head down-field to remove the linebackers and safety men from the scene of activities. Assuming that the timing is perfect, the best that the opponent can do is to grab the ball carrier and employ an arm tackle instead of a full shoulder tackle, in which case a back with the correct amount of determination and fortitude may get away from defenders many times in the course of an afternoon. Man-for-man blocking enables blocking assignments to be switched very quickly at the line of scrimmage with a minimum number of men having to make the change.

Lucrative rewards result from perfect timing and faking. Our men learn that it is much easier to fake a man out of position than to block him out. The linemen soon know whether or not their backs are faking correctly. If the back makes a good fake, the defensive lineman will take a step, and at that time the offensive lineman should move in fast and block his opponent out of the play. A thing that we always like to see in our movies is that the faking back who does not have the ball is being tackled. Oftentimes during our 1947 season our left halfback, Terry Brennan, 165 pounder from Milwaukee, was hit very hard at the line of scrimmage because he had exe-cuted a perfect fake that allowed the ball carrier to get away to a quick and unmolested start.

The spreads that we mentioned earlier widen the defense, thus allowing passes to go for longer gains before the oppo-nents can get to the receiver. Adequate pass protection is ob-tained more easily as a result of all of the faking that occurs close to the line of scrimmage. This deception momentarily freezes the defense and allows for longer gains when a pass is faked, followed immediately by a run.

In the "T," less wear and tear on the personnel is evident in view of the fact that each play is over in such a short space of time. Our offense is arranged to function regardless of the defense, since we find that a different defense faces us almost every Saturday. When we run into something new, our quarterback starts right off with our "bread and butter" plays, keeping his eyes open for weaknesses and getting reports from the men-in-motion. Before too long, we find that the enemy has some vulnerable spot, which when hit causes them to change to a more normal defense. As soon as they do this we start operating at full speed.

The spectators like the motion. The "T" is a democratic formation that utilizes all of the backs at all times. Because of its flexibility the "T" pays large dividends on good quarterbacking. The field general has an opportunity to use to a greater advantage the outstanding characteristics of all the players at the same time. For instance, one of your backs may be a terrific faker and another a very good runner; by utilizing these two assets in one play, the signal caller can definitely confuse the opponents and make it easier for his own linemen. He usually ends up with a substantial gain for the team.

We can prevent concentration of defenders by spreading an end and a motion back in the same area. This forces man-for-man coverage, which gives the offense a big advantage because they know where the ball is going and can cause the opponents to have three defenders on the opposite side of the gridiron.

REQUISITES FOR A SUCCESSFUL "T" FORMATION

A football coach should analyze his material carefully before making a change to the "T." First, as in all of our requirements, the squad members must possess a burning desire to win. Second, look to your quarterback, for he is the heart and soul of the "T" formation. On the signal caller rest all of your hopes of success. An offense is no better than its quarterback. He must possess: (a) brains, (b) fortitude, (c) a terrific amount of competitive spirit, since his spirit permeates the entire team, (d) strong powers of concentration, because he must be able to visualize in a split second a play that will succeed, and (e) a fine character; he must: (f) be an excellent ball handler—if he played basketball, all the better, (g) learn the "T" completely, (h) and be a sixty-minute battler. Third, we need fast-charging linemen in the "T" who know their assignments from A to Z. Downfield blocking is the key to scoring success in the "T"; therefore, you need men in the line who can get out fast and keep abreast of your backs as they head toward pay territory. An incident we like to recall in this regard occurred at the time Emil "Red" Sitko ran seventy-six yards to score our second touchdown against Southern California in 1947. It was a simple off-end play and "Red" really had to battle with the Trojan linebacker to shake loose from his arm tackle, but he had the character and fortitude to do so and was on his way downfield. When he was about ten yards past the line of scrimmage he was joined by George Connor and Bill Fischer, our left tackle and left guard, who escorted him along the sidelines. At about the twenty-yard line George dropped off the caravan to obliterate a would-be tackler, while Bill kept Emil from having a hand laid on him as they went into the end zone together. Both of the above linemen weigh over 220 pounds, but they possessed that burning desire to see their teammate in the end zone, so they drove themselves to accompany him all the way.

At Notre Dame we ask our backs to drive hard and come in tall when they take the ball from the quarterback. Their timing must be perfect, which we shall discuss when we get to the individual positions. Your backs must have implicit confidence in your quarterback. If they know he is going to feed the ball perfectly, then they can go about their faking without peeking to see how the ball handler is doing. We over exaggerate our fakes in practice in order to perfect them for game time. Backfield men must relax; tense men fumble too often.

When your offense is running smoothly, do not enjoy it, but analyze the situation and find out why it is going so well and against what enemy mistakes the quarterbacking is paying off. Always know these causes, since they may be present in a far different form in your next game. When you see the opponents make a mistake, be certain that you never make the same one. The attitude must be present in every man on every play that "If I fail to carry out my individual assignment perfectly, the play cannot succeed." If this general all-around determination is prevalent and it combines with good physical condition, loyalty, confidence, and unselfishness, then I believe that you will find it takes a mighty good team to defeat you.

BASIC FUNDAMENTALS OF THE "T"

Since first installing this system at Notre Dame, we have used various types of huddles. Experience has proven to us that the one diagrammed on page 19 is best in all respects. We spend a great deal of time on the huddle because we believe that this phase must be perfected in order to get in more plays per minute. The team that runs the most plays has the best chance of scoring the most points. With this in mind, we drill our men individually as to how they can use time in the huddle to distinct advantage. The plan is divided into three steps.

First, the center assumes a position eight to ten yards behind the ball just as soon as the previous play is completed. He raises high his right hand, calling loudly to his teammates, who immediately fall into position around him, as illustrated. From his vantage point at the end of the huddle the signal caller can look over the entire situation while the other players are assuming their positions. As soon as the huddle is formed the quarterback steps in—knowing at this point what play he intends to call. He should look directly at the left end and call the play crisply and clearly, articulating each word so that his teammates may read his lips if the wind is blowing.

Second, as soon as the quarterback has called the play we move into the next step. The quarterback says, "Turn," at which time all the linemen turn out from the center with the left end moving up next to the left tackle at the same time the quarterback moves over behind the center. The right end steps directly behind the quarterback and assumes his normal position.

The center waits two full seconds before calling "Up," which initiates step three. At this point the linemen move swiftly up to the line of scrimmage, with the center assuming his position over the ball. The reason for the two-second delay is to give the linemen an opportunity to analyze the defense. We ask them to look the situation over carefully, bearing in mind what play has been called and what they think the best blocking assignment would be.

Now we have the center over the ball ready to go. Never

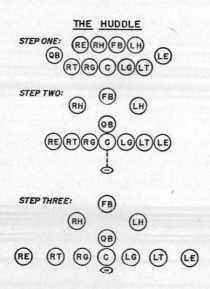

THE HUDDLE

vary in this aspect, since you may want to run a play on "hike," in which case your center would not be tipping off the play by getting into his position immediately.   The guards should assume their position about eight inches from the center, the tackles must be one foot from the guards, while the ends line up one yard out from the tackles.   All linemen, with the exception of the center, should have their hands on their knees with a little weight on the palms of their hands and one foot behind the other.   In the backfield each halfback should line up three and one-half yards behind the line of scrimmage, each with the respective tackle's inside foot directly ahead. The fullback's position is directly behind the quarterback and six inches farther back than the halfbacks.

As soon as the linemen are in position the quarterback calls "Get—down."   The "get" is just a preliminary message to inform the team that the "down" is coming.   On hearing the latter word, the linemen should make certain that they set themselves in an advantageous blocking angle.   We firmly believe that the best blocking angle can be obtained when the offensive lineman is six inches away from his target.   If the man is any further away from his target, he will have to lunge.   In regard to the stance at this stage, it will vary with the individual man.   He knows what his job is and how he can best perform the task.   On the "down," the backs should line up with one foot slightly behind the other.   If they do not do this, you will find them taking one step backward before moving up to take the ball from the quarterback.

NUMBERING SYSTEM

We believe it would be prudent for the reader to acquaint himself thoroughly with the following system of numbering, since we plan to use it exclusively throughout the book.   Since our center is our pivot man, that is the spot where we start

to number our holes.   The right hip of the center is hole number one, right hip of the right guard is hole number three, right hip of the right tackle hole number five, right hip of the right end hole number seven, while hole number nine is far outside the right end.   Starting again with the center, we number our holes on the left side with even numbers.   The pivot man's left hip is zero, and so on out to number eight, which is far outside the left end.

We give numbers to six men on our team.   These six men are the ones who are potential ball carriers—the two ends and the four backfield men.   The quarterback draws number one, the left halfback two, the fullback three, the right halfback four, the right end five, and the left end is number six.   As a result of the given numbers, when the quarterback calls play number "43," it simply means that the number four back is to carry the ball through the number three hole.   We sometimes say "43—25," which means the same play will be run with the number two back going in motion and that the ball will be snapped on the fifth count.   The halfback will always go in motion to the same side as that to which the play is being run unless the quarterback adds "opposite" after the "25."   An amusing incident arose in our Tulane game in 1946 when George Ratterman, now one of the outstanding quarterbacks in professional football, called "43—45," which meant that the right half was to go through the number three hole, and also the right half was to go in motion.   Our number four back took one look at Tulane's big tackle and decided to go in motion.   George, after making a perfect fake to the back who wasn't there, ran for a gain of twelve yards.   This proves that George Ratterman was not only a very quick thinker but also a great opportunist, as he has conclusively proven many times since to fans of professional football.

The blocking assignments are called by the tackles.   We started out by having the quarterback call them but found that the tackles are in a better position to determine the angles

available.   We have achieved better results by having these all-important decisions made by the linemen.   The most critical man on defense is the onside linebacker; that is, the man backing up the line on the side to which we plan to run the play.   Anyone in the line may go through and block this man or we may ask a lineman to pull out and come around on him.

For many obvious reasons we do not plan to give our exact blocking calls, and we sincerely hope that you will understand why.   However, we do plan to describe each and every move that our blockers make and how we set up our blocking assignments against all types of defenses.   In the chapters dealing with plays we will diagram each of our "bread and butter" plays against different types of defensive set-ups.   We will then go on to show and explain what each man does, and later, in the chapters on individual positions, we will explain how he does the blocking.

Both tackles call an assignment immediately after the quarterback says "Down," but naturally the onside tackle is the only one the lads listen to, the other being for decoy purposes. If the tackle sees that the hole is clogged up, he will simply say "Up two," or some similar phrase, which would mean that a "43" play would become a "45."   If the defense shifts to the play side, he might say "Cancel," which would cause the quarterback to call "Opposite" or some code name that would run the opposite of the original play.   The opposite of "43" is "22"; that is, instead of the right halfback going off the right guard, the left halfback carries the ball off the left guard.   When teaching a play to our squad we always give them the opposite at the same time, since we want the two plays thought of on the same plane at the same time.

In regard to the offside linebacker, we usually have our center or offside guard take care of him.   This assignment is decided upon between these two men at the line of scrimmage. The usual procedure is to have a code whereby the center just

calls the guard's name when he wants him to go through for the linebacker. If the center calls out his own name, then he plans to go through and block the aforementioned opponent.

In concluding this chapter and before entering the section on plays, we should like to draw a diagram that will illustrate all of the numbering assignments as explained previously in this chapter. The charts will give you the number of each hole as well as the numbers we assign to each of our potential ball carriers.

Numbers of holes and players:

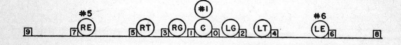

Distance chart:

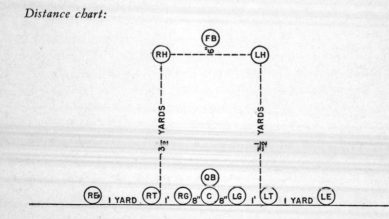

3

The Quick-Opener

THE "T" FORMATION is based on the element of surprise, and to my way of thinking there is no better way to capitalize on this element than to have an operation completed before the enemy realizes what is happening. This is what play number "43" does for us. It is the most basic play in our system and also the most used play in our plan of attack. Play "43" and its opposite "22" have gained more yardage for us, since we installed this system, than have any other plays. I sincerely believe that the reason many coaches are not having success with the "T" is that they look upon this play as being too elementary for them to waste their time on it. In order for any other plays to work successfully from this formation, we believe that it is absolutely essential that the opponent always be tensed to expect a quick-opener. If you have them in this frame of mind, you will find it much easier to make them go after a good fake. In reviewing our seasons' movies, we see innumerable instances where we have faked a "43" or "22" and the faking halfback has been hit hard by overanxious linemen in their zealous attempt to halt our basic plays. We like to have our quarterbacks run these plays many times during the course of every game, because oftentimes after the first period we find that the enemy tends to relax a bit, and it is at this time that our halfbacks can break through and into the clear before the linebackers react to what is going on.

We have a set pattern for our halfback to follow after he goes through the line on this play. Naturally, circumstances may cause him to deviate from this plan, but we ask our ball carrier, if possible, to go through the line for approximately five yards and then cut in the direction away from the hole side of the line. That is, on a "43" the halfback cuts to his left, and on a "22" he cuts to his right. Our reason for this is to permit the offside end and tackle to get downfield ahead of the man with the ball, and give him some assistance with the enemy backfield men.

Play "43," as mentioned earlier, means the number four back through the number three hole. This play may be run with either the left halfback or the fullback in motion or out on a flanker, or the quarterback may choose to spread an end just to disconcert the men across the line. The success of this play depends mainly on the timing that is employed by the quarterback and the ball carrier. It works so fast that they must meet perfectly in order to avoid a fumble. Work on this exchange in practice until your men can perform it without the slightest hesitation. (See photos of this play following page 132.)

ASSIGNMENTS FOR THE QUICK-OPENER

On page 26 we will diagram this quick-opening play against a normal six-man line, showing both "22" and "43," and showing the blocking assignments we use when we run up against such a defense. Since this defense is the one we most commonly face, we have devised two methods of approaching it, with the best method being decided upon at the line of scrimmage by the onside tackle. Many times the linebacker will move just as the quarterback starts to call "Down," and it is then that the tackle may decide which of our two plans will work out most advantageously.

"43" AGAINST A NORMAL SIX-MAN LINE

As can be seen in the diagram, we have the defensive tackle lined up on the head of our ends; that is, directly opposite our flanker men.   When "43" is called and the right tackle sees

"43" Against a normal six-man line:

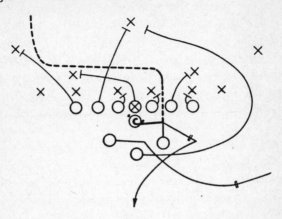

"22" Against a normal six-man line:

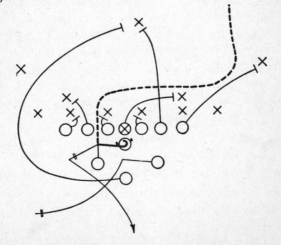

a situation such as this at the line of scrimmage, he usually feels that our right end has a more advantageous blocking angle on the opposing tackle than he has. Thus, he would call a blocking assignment that would send the end directly at the tackle while he, himself, would go through and block the onside linebacker away from the hole. We shall now give the assignments exactly as we give them to our squad members every time we diagram a play for them. We go from end to end and then through the entire backfield.

We call upon the *right end* to shoulder block the defensive left tackle toward the sidelines. He should keep driving him out until he is certain that the halfback is through the hole and down the field. When this duty is performed he must head downfield himself to see if he can do some constructive blocking.

Our *right tackle* must spring out toward the linebacker. We ask him to head as if he were going past the man to get the halfback, and then he should cut back fast and bury his shoulder deep in the opponent's midsection. Our tackles continue to block the man until they are absolutely certain he can be of no harm to the play.

The *right guard* must get a fast charge at the man on his head and drive him away from the hole. He should be careful not to let the man pivot away from him or he may close up the hole. This defender is the closest man to the hole, and we want him to have to go across the line of scrimmage in order to get away from our guard's blocking.

The *center* starts to sprint as soon as the ball leaves his hands. He sprints through the line until he is a little bit deeper than the offside linebacker. As that man starts to move over into the play, our pivot man blocks him back toward the line of scrimmage. The play is coming in his direction, so the center must make certain that this man is kept out of the play for a length of time sufficient to allow the halfback to be on his way.

Our *left guard* blocks the defensive guard away from the hole. We ask him to stay with the opponent for three full counts before releasing his block and heading downfield in the general direction of the ball carrier, looking for anyone who is wearing the wrong colored shirt.

The *left tackle* is a downfield blocker on this type of play. He must not arrive there too soon or he will not be able to keep the safety man occupied long enough for the halfback to get free. He should wait until the man with the ball catches up with him and then place himself between the ball carrier and the opponent. The block should never be made until the enemy is right next to him because a full body block is most effective on the important man. We tell our blockers that if they will stay with the ball carrier the potential tacklers will come to them.

The *left end* employs the same tactics as were outlined for the left tackle on downfield blocking. His man is the defensive right halfback, toward whom he should run, never allowing that man to get near the number four back.

The position of the *quarterback*'s feet is designated by the little dots on the diagram. Many coaches think this is a tip-off as to which direction the play will run, so we often vary it with the play. Upon receiving the ball from the center, the quarterback does a reverse pivot (which will be explained in detail in the chapter on quarterback play) and feeds the ball to the right halfback. As soon as the ball carrier is away, the quarterback keeps his hands in close to his stomach while he takes two steps out toward the opponent's goal line. The two little lines indicate a fake pitchout that he makes to the left halfback. After faking very hard to that back, he then fades back and throws a fake pass. All of this time he has his back at least partially facing the line of scrimmage so the opponent cannot see what is going on. This is absolutely necessary if the ball carrier is to get through the hole before the play is diagnosed.

The *left halfback* steps off with his left foot and then cuts on a ninety-degree angle to his right. He sprints over until he is behind the center and then starts to "belly" back. When the quarterback fakes the pitchout the number two back must fake right with him in order to confuse the enemy. Note the two little lines crossing his path. We spend as much time as possible on good faking and have many hints that we believe will prove helpful in teaching halfbacks to fake properly.

The *right halfback* must start like a shot out of a cannon. As the play begins to unfold, he eyes the quarterback with split vision until he is ready to receive the ball. He then looks down and follows it right into the pocket. We tell our ball carriers to grasp the ball, seize it, tuck it away, and move it downfield. Once he has the ball in his possession, he bolts through the line for about five yards before cutting to his left, where he picks up his blockers.

Our *fullback* must "fly" out to the sidelines, keeping a constant watch to see just who, if anyone, follows him. He should do this with an eye toward what play, similar to "43," would work if he were to go out there all alone.

"22" AGAINST A NORMAL SIX-MAN LINE

The opposite of "43," which is "22," is always taught at the same time. In the diagram for the latter play you will notice that we use the identical set-up, except that we have the left tackle call the blocking assignments, and it is his duty to sprint through the line to block the onside linebacker. The quarterback's feet are in exactly the opposite position, and he does a reverse pivot to his right, coming around and feeding his left halfback just about two yards behind the line of scrimmage. It was on this simple "22" that Bob Livingstone shook loose to run ninety-two yards against the University of Southern California in the Los Angeles Coliseum at the close of our 1947 season. At this time I should like to mention a word about Bob Livingstone, who was one of our greatest sophomores in 1942, and who left shortly after that season closed to put in more than three years in the U. S. Army infantry. When Bob came back in 1946 he found it very difficult to make his legs react as they formerly had, but he worked doggedly at it, never giving up, although at times he looked like but a shadow of his 1942 self. However, this determination paid great dividends; late in the 1947 season his legs came into shape, and he starred for Notre Dame in our games with Navy, Army, Tulane, and shone the brightest in his last game for the "Fighting Irish" in sunny California.

QUICK-OPENER AGAINST A TIGHTENED SIX-MAN LINE

On page 31 we have outlined the very same play against the same kind of a defense, except that it is pulled in a little tighter, which brings the defensive tackle into the slot between our right end and tackle. When the enemy makes this change after our tackle has already called the blocking assignments, all that is necessary is for him to say "X" for exchange, and he and the end exchange assignments without causing the slightest mixup.

Against this defense we have our onside tackle drive the defensive tackle out toward the sidelines and our end come around behind the tackle and meet the linebacker as he is coming in on the play. The reason for having the end pull behind the tackle is to draw the linebacker into the play and make certain that the hole is opened first. The assignments of all the other linemen remain the same on this version of "43."

In running "22" against this defense, there are the same changes as in "43" plus one other minor difference. The defensive right guard is now at an angle that would make it much easier for the center to block him than to have the guard do the job. All the center need do is call out his own name, which will send the guard through after the linebacker, and the pivot man can take care of the guard. The remaining players go about their assignments in the same manner as they did in the previous play.

When the man with the ball arrives at the line he must ex-

"43" Against a normal six-man line with the defensive tackle in the gap between the offensive end and tackle:

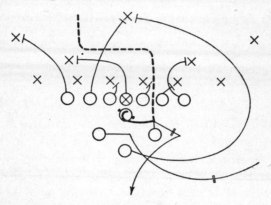

"22" Against a normal six-man line with the defensive tackle in the gap between the offensive end and tackle:

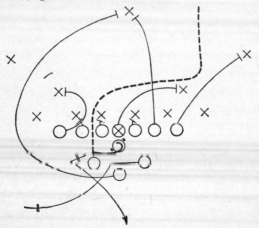

pect not always to be able to drive a truck through the hole. It may be small, or it may be off to one side or the other, but he must use it and make the best of it.   One of the finest examples of such opportunism was given by Larry Coutre, our second string right halfback, during the 1947 game with Army.   Notre Dame was on Army's twelve-yard line when Larry was called upon to carry the ball on a "45."   When he hit the line there was no hole whatsoever.   He just stopped dead, cut sharply to his right, and sprinted into the end zone before the Army linemen had recovered.

QUICK-OPENER AGAINST THE 5-3-2-1

A 5-3-2-1 defense places a man directly on the head of our center, and this man is in the most advantageous position to break up our quick-opening plays.   Therefore, we "double team" him, which means we assign both our center and our right guard to insure that he does not stop the ball carrier's forward progress.   On page 33 our quick-opener is diagrammed against this type of defense.

The *right end* should immediately sprint out to get the onside linebacker.   If he moves fast enough, the end should be able to drive the enemy all the way to the sidelines.   The angle is fairly good and the defender is far enough away from the hole for our man to work deliberately.

Ask the *right tackle* to come across the line of scrimmage; that is, he should step quickly across so that the opposing tackle will stay on his right side.   This will make the block much easier and will be away from the hole.

The *right guard* and *center* must double team the man playing opposite the center.   As soon as one of these men is in a position to handle the enemy alone, the other lineman should head on downfield to help out in whatever situation develops.

Our *left guard* must pull around very fast behind the right guard. He takes short digging steps as he buries his shoulder in the midsection of the center linebacker. We insist that he stick with that man until the play is well on down the grid-iron.

The *left tackle* and *left end* are asked once again to take care of the downfield blocking assignments. Before they break away they must make certain that none of the opponents are pulling back to stop the play. All of our downfield blockers are instructed never to pass up a potential tackler.

"43" Against the 5-3-2-1:

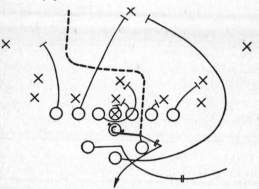

"22" Against the 5-3-2-1:

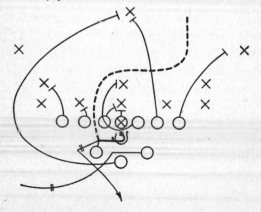

We want the field cleared, and if anyone makes a tackle, we want it to be a man in front of our blockers rather than a man behind them.

All four *backs* follow exactly the same procedure on this play as when we oppose a six-man line. However, we frequently send our left halfback in motion with the hope that the onside linebacker will follow him out, thus allowing our right end to be an additional downfield blocker. We try to achieve this at every opportunity, because the more blockers we have past the line of scrimmage, the better the chance of obtaining six points.

Hereafter we will not explain the opposites of each play, since in each case they are identical except that it is the corresponding man on the other side of the center who is carrying out the assignments.

"43" AGAINST AN OVERSHIFTED SIX-MAN LINE

A six-man line that is overshifted to the hole side gives us a chance to use cross blocking. As shown in the diagram on page 35, such a shift requires the halfback to veer a bit toward the right after he gets through the hole in order to circle the defensive guard. When a cross block is called, we ask the tackle to go first because his man, being nearest the hole, is most dangerous. Also, the man who is to be blocked by our guard will have partially committed himself, thus making him an easier target. Since changing to the "T" we have found this to be a common defense, especially when the right halfback is the best running back. It is a tough defense to crack, but if your ball carrier can get through the line and make a fast cut, he will find that he has plenty of assistance once he gets past the linebackers.

The *right end* is asked to cut over fast and double team with the left guard on the center linebacker. They must drive this man toward the line of scrimmage and out in the direction of the sidelines. He will prove extremely troublesome if they do not get the jump on him. Once he starts retreating, one man can take care of him and the other should release his block and join in the downfield maneuvers.

When cross blocking is called, the *right tackle* goes first and buries his shoulder in the defensive left guard. He should

"43" Against a six-man line overshifted to the right:

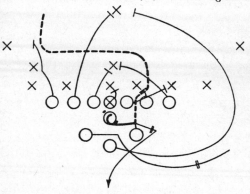

"22" Against a six-man line overshifted to the left:

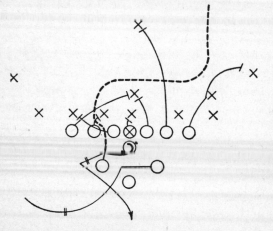

continue to take short, digging steps until he is absolutely certain that the ball carrier is well on his way.   We instruct our men to be especially careful that the opponent does not roll away from them and bring the ball carrier down from behind. If the guard makes a move, we want him to have to circle our tackle to his left, which will bring him into the backfield after the ball has left.

Our *right guard* hesitates for a split second to allow the tackle to cross in front of him.   Once the tackle is past, he moves over rapidly, giving the defensive tackle an inside head fake, and then blocking from the outside with his shoulder. He should keep bumping his man away from the line of fire. This type of block should give our guard a very good opportunity to shake up this man, and he should not miss this chance, for it is at times like this that we have a real opportunity to ruin a man's desire to participate in a football contest. When that spirit is broken, touchdowns come easily.

The *center* has a man playing directly opposite him, and we ask him to block that man away from the hole.   We want him to stick with his opponent for quite some time, since we usually find the man in that position to be exceptionally aggressive.   As previously explained, the *left guard* double teams with the right end on the center linebacker.   He should render all the assistance possible in order to get the job done more quickly.

Our *left tackle* lopes through for the safety man.   He should not turn on his speed until the ball carrier has caught up with him.   He should always try to keep about a step ahead of the man with the ball, and about three yards away from him.   He is joined in the downfield blocking by the *left end,* who first shoulder brushes the offside linebacker.   Should this backer-up be exceptionally aggressive, we ask our end to stay with him as long as is necessary.

The activities of the *backfield men* do not change against this type of defense; however, we frequently have the quarterback send a flanker to the opposite side from that to which he intends to run the play. When you do this, scrutinize the changes that are made in the defense. Often you will find that this causes the break for which you have been waiting, especially if the right halfback is the mainstay of your offensive unit. On a team where the left halfback is the number one ball carrier, play number "22" takes precedence over "43," but all of the foregoing suggestions hold true. We like to run both plays as often as possible, to prevent the enemy from formulating a set defense.

Many times when we meet an overshifted defense we have found that it is easier on the linemen if the *right end* crosses over and blocks the defensive guard in, and the *right tackle* goes through to work on the middle linebacker. This works out best when the opposing guard is playing directly on the head of the tackle. In this situation it would be too difficult for the offensive tackle to assume a good angle; therefore, he just informs the end of the exchange of assignments and the remaining players carry out their original duties. Cases like this have proved to us that the tackles are in the best position to call the blocking assignments. This is a far cry from the days when all that was required of a tackle was that he be big and strong. We were extremely fortunate in 1947 when we had two of the outstanding tackles in college football. Our Captain, George Connor, and his running mate, Zig Czarobski, were picked on many All-American teams throughout the country. These two men were quick thinkers who always tried to get the job done the fastest way, even though many times it meant burying themselves in obscurity rather than performing conspicuously so that the fans could notice their performance. With these outstanding linemen calling our blocking assignments, we found that every member of our team had the utmost confidence in their ability, and, consequently, each man carried out his own individual job to the best of his ability.

"43" AGAINST A SEVEN-MAN LINE

All things being equal, the quick-opener in the "T" formation should work most successfully against a seven-man line.   The reason for this is that with man-for-man blocking, we find that each opponent in this defensive set-up is in a position where he can be blocked with the least difficulty. It is against this defense that the timing must be most perfect, and if it is, you will find that it brings excellent results. We find that the men react more quickly against this defense because it is much easier to recognize.   The individual assignments are simple and a brief outline should clarify all duties.

The *right end* blocks the defensive tackle away from the hole while the *right tackle* is driving the opposing guard in the same direction.   The tackle should make certain that he gets a good angle when the quarterback calls "Down," since once he has the angle he will not have much trouble moving the man out.   A shoulder block should be applied, and we ask him to stay with the man long enough to allow the ball carrier to be far down the field.

The key blocker on this play is the *right guard*. He should make a very hard fake at the defensive center, then circle the linebacker, and drive the latter man back and away from the hole.   A quick-starting, hard-driving guard can make this play a "breadwinner" against a seven-man line.   His fake should make the enemy center an easy target for our *pivot man*, who blocks him with his left shoulder.

The *left guard's* duty is to see that the opposing guard has to pass on his left if he wants to get into our backfield.   If he does this, enough time will elapse to allow the ball carrier to be on his way.   The *left end* and *left tackle* are once again called upon to do the downfield blocking; however, we do ask them to scuffle with the opposing linemen long enough to prevent them from pulling out and catching up with the runner. If the line appears to be too tight to open a hole, we usually will spread our onside end, which will cause the defense to expand.

"43" Against a normal seven-man line:

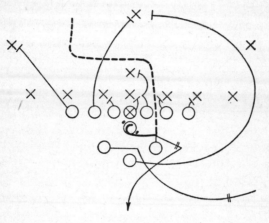

"22" Against a normal seven-man line:

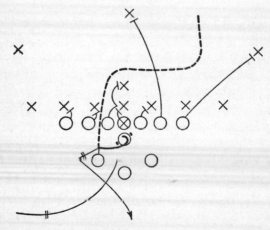

"43" AGAINST A SLANTING SIX-MAN LINE

The sixth type of defense that we look at many times on a Saturday afternoon is what appears to be a normal six-man line, but which we observe, as the signals are being called, is a line that slants to such an extent that it would be impossible for our linemen to do a satisfactory blocking job.   It took a long time to solve this because we had difficulty in locating just where the men were.   After running through our movies a number of times we analyzed the defense as diagrammed on page 41, and since have had considerable success with the blocking tactics given to combat it.   We have given this defense a code name, and when our opponents slide into it during a game, our tackle simply announces that name and the men automatically go about their business.

The *right end* has an assignment that is entirely dependent upon the position he assumes as he gets down into the line. His job is to block the defensive tackle away from the hole — his best approach is to allow the man to step across the line, then to force his shoulder into him and keep him moving in the desired direction.   The *right tackle* must block the onside guard completely out of the hole before the back comes roaring through.   A good block by this man is the makings of a successful play.

Our *right guard* has the all-important task of riding the onside linebacker away from the hole.   He crosses over immediately after the tackle moves, and maneuvers himself behind the backer-up. We do not allow him to circle his own tackle, but we want him to cross over exactly where the tackle lined up.   He should make extensive use of the head fake because the defensive man has a good opportunity to see him coming.   The *center* sprints through for about five yards before cutting back to employ the element of surprise in blocking the offside linebacker. When the play is past, the center should release his block and go goalward.

Our *left guard* blocks the man on his head away from the hole while the remaining members of the team carry out the

"43" Against a slanting six-man line:

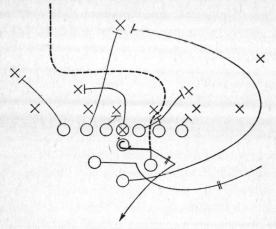

"22" Against a slanting six-man line:

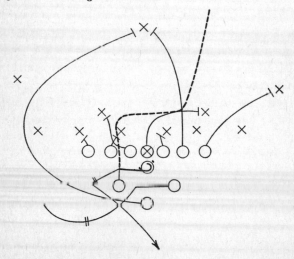

same assignments as given against a normal six-man line. We should like to suggest that the coaches pay particular attention to this defense, since they will find that if they install some plan for coping with such variations, they will have a weapon that can be much more potent than anything formulated against a positive defense, without allowing for slight changes. A code word should be agreed upon to cover such a slanting set-up.

HELPFUL HINTS ON THE QUICK-OPENER

Plays "43" and "22" are to the "T" formation what a left jab is to a boxer; that is, the first sturdy stone of a solid foundation. Without these plays you do not have the "T" in its true form. Some of the things that we have found to contribute a great deal to the success of these plays are given here.

We notice that if our linemen can possibly block high without interfering with their effectiveness, it adds to the deception. The actions of a good quarterback are hard to follow under any conditions, but they are much more confusing if the opponent is trying to analyze them through a 220-pound lineman. We do not ask our key blockers to worry about concealing the backs, but we do like to have our offside linemen come up fast to screen the activities behind the line.

The guards must be exceptionally careful not to step back even one inch or they will interfere with the quarterback's pivot. This must be doubly guarded against when the guard is pulling to do some cross blocking. It is a tendency common among linemen, but if properly trained, they will overcome it.

The right halfback is the principal man on the play, and it is absolutely essential that he and the quarterback work together without a flaw. He should take the ball on his left side, right at the hip, as he is striding forward with his right foot. The reason that his left leg must be back is to allow the quarterback to lay the ball in the pocket without the pocket forcing itself upon the ball. Right halfbacks should practice taking the ball with just their left hand, and when they can do this at full speed, they should start using both hands. This will give them confidence in their ability to receive the ball. We have found that whenever a fumble occurs on this play, it is usually due to the fact that the halfback starts reaching for the ball, or he is coming in too low. He must stand high enough to form a good pocket for the quarterback to find.

When new linemen are assigned to block downfield, they want to get right down there and obliterate the defensive backs. This is an admirable trait, but oftentimes they head downfield when many opponents are still standing near the line of scrimmage. We tell our men never to pass up an opponent unless he is on his back. Such plays as these were not devised to score a touchdown every time they are called; therefore, the blockers must clear the field step by step.

We drill our tackles on the blocking calls by putting them in a room with a blackboard and asking them to turn their backs to the board. We then sketch all types of defenses on the board and call a tackle by name. As soon as he turns, we point to one of the defenses and ask that he call the blocking assignment just as quickly as possible. You will notice that many coaches today are using different tackles on offense than they use on defense, and it is our belief that their offensive tackle is the quicker thinker of the two. This should be a daily routine, taking only about ten minutes. Do not let the men tire of such a drill.

If any person were to pick up a list of Notre Dame statistics for the seasons of 1946, 1947, and 1948, he would notice that the name of Emil Sitko was listed right at the top of the heap for average gain per try. Emil was our number one right halfback during those years, and we would be willing to wager that more than fifty percent of his ball carrying was on this simple, quick-opening play. The play is easy to teach, takes very little time to carry out, and employs the element of surprise to the "nth" degree; it is our firm conviction that no coach, the writer included, uses this "bread and butter" play to its fullest advantage.   Human nature causes men to want to try something new and different and thus to forsake the old standbys.   This is as true in football as it is in every other walk of life.   However, I do believe that when we get down close to the goal line we get as much out of these basic "T" plays as does anyone with whom we have come in contact.

The main thought we should like to impress upon the coaches as we leave this play is that if they will drill each man until he knows this play perfectly, they will find little difficulty in teaching him the other plays of the "T" formation.

4

Sweeping the End

WE CALL THIS play "29H," and it has produced more thrilling moments for the Notre Dame football fans than has any other play in our entire attack. The call number signifies that the number two back, that is, the left halfback, is going to carry the ball through the number nine hole, which is the outside hole on the right. The "H" means that our other halfback is faking, and in this instance he is faking a complete "43." The success of this play depends very much upon the ability of the right halfback to execute a perfect "43" without receiving the ball.

It was this play that Gerry Cowhig carried out so well in our now immortal scoreless game with West Point in Yankee Stadium back in 1946. Gerry was one of the leading ground gainers that afternoon, and it was this play that aided us so much. Since it is not especially adaptable to actual scoring drives, we were unable to make use of it when we approached close enough to see the goal posts. It is a simple play that we always call after our left halfback notices that the defense is not paying too much attention to him when he makes his fake on play number "43."

ASSIGNMENTS FOR SWEEPING THE END

"29H" AGAINST A NORMAL SIX-MAN LINE

When we run into a 6-2-2-1 defense, we ask our *right end* to brush block the defensive left end and then lope downfield,

45

getting himself a good angle on their defensive left halfback so that he can stop him as he attempts to come over and slow down the man with the ball. We ask him to make certain that their end plays him a little before he moves downfield.

"29H" against a normal six-man line:

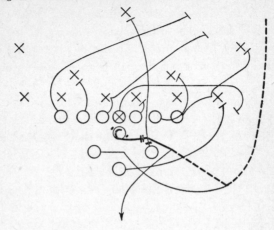

"48H" against a normal six-man line:

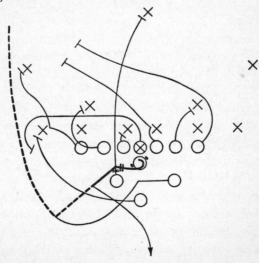

Our *right tackle,* keeping high, pulls around behind the spot where the right end was lined up. He makes it appear as if he were going past the linebacker and then cuts back on him and drives him in toward the line of scrimmage. On this play we ask our onside tackle to disobey one of the cardinal rules for good offensive play—that is, "Stay as low as you can as long as you can." Our reason for asking the tackle to come up tall is so that he will screen the quarterback's activities behind the line, thus making it that much more difficult for the defense to determine whether or not the ball is given to the right half-back.

The *right guard* has a man on his head, and we ask him to block this man away from the hole. He should scuffle with his opponent for three full counts and then move on into the front lines. As soon as the ball leaves the *center's* hands, he should take about three steps straight forward and cut on a ninety-degree angle toward the sidelines. When he gets outside of their left end he cuts back and blocks anyone who is approaching the play from the rear. Ever so many times we find that opposing linemen who have been fooled by the fake are in an advantageous position to come up on the ball carrier from the rear. Hence, we ask our center to see to it that no one enters his area. As in all our plays, if the center finds that he would have a better angle to block the defensive guard than does our guard, he calls the guard's name and the latter will cut through and block back.

The *left guard* blocks his man very hard, but does not waste any time with him. After he has made his contact with the man, he should streak for the sidelines and see of what assistance he can be to the left halfback as he heads for the goal line. Whenever this play comes to our mind, we like to think of Fred Rovai, who was a guard on our 1946 National Championship team and co-captain in our game with Southern California at the conclusion of that season. Notre Dame was having a little difficulty in getting rolling until George Ratterman, who was quarterbacking at the time, called "29H" with Coy McGee running from the left halfback slot. Coy was making his way downfield very well until it looked as if he were completely hemmed in by the red shirted Trojans. It was at this instant that a big green jersey with the number 42 very prominent on its back seemed to take command. Once again McGee was in the open and Fred Rovai was clearing the field ahead of him, although he outweighed McGee by approximately seventy pounds.

The *left tackle's* job can be simple if he works at it correctly. He must keep the offside linebacker from crossing over toward the line of fire. A thing to be remembered is that, as a rule, linebackers are fairly fast, and quite a bit of time elapses while the ball is in the backfield, which may allow this man to move over toward the ball. Therefore, we ask our tackle to stick with him until he is positive that he cannot be of any danger to the ball carrier. The *left end* pulls fast in order to get downfield to block for the ball carrier. He should try to make the linebacker think he is coming at him, which will make things easier for the tackle.

The *quarterback* must fake perfectly to the right halfback after making his reverse pivot. He carries out every minute detail of play number "43" until it comes to the actual releasing of the ball. He does all of his faking close to the line of scrimmage. He rides the ball into the halfback's stomach, staying low for leverage and deception. As he pulls away from the halfback, he brings his left shoulder high to cover the movements of his hands. While he is making the fake his right foot will be advanced. As soon as the back is past, he takes two steps and laterals out to the left halfback. We ask our quarterbacks to squeeze the ball out with lots of wrist action and very little arm energy. He should stand tall when he releases the ball, because this will tend to send it on a straight path rather than an upward trend. Fast steps will put momentum into the lateral without the use of any arm movement.   The ball should be released from the man's waist.

As soon as the ball is snapped, the *left halfback* should start to sprint toward the sidelines.   When he gets behind the center he should start to "belly" back and get as far away as possible before the quarterback laterals the ball.   The reason for the "bellying" is to give a better passing angle to the quarterback.   We instruct our lads never to reach for the ball if it is coming in correctly.   They should "look" the ball all the way into their hands, turning only at the neck.   One satisfactory method we have employed in order to guarantee that our halfbacks will "look" the ball into their hands is to number all of our footballs.   When a lateral is caught we stop the play immediately and ask what the number on the ball is, without allowing the man to glance down.   We find that in a short time all of our lateral catchers are following the required procedure.

A good *right halfback* can contribute more to the success of this play than can be imagined.   When he comes in to fake with the quarterback he should turn his body to the left to screen the maneuvers from the defensive end and tackle.   As soon as the signal caller pulls the ball away he should double up and start churning through the line.   We like to see our faking halfback tackled, since we have noticed that whenever he is stopped the ball carrier gets away for a substantial gain. The *fullback* sweeps toward the sidelines, blocking the first enemy out of the path.   If the defensive end has gone for our end's fake, the fullback goes right on past him.

Another successful method of running this play against the same defense is to spread the right end wide, which puts him in a more advantageous spot to brush block the opposing end without delay.   The more you use the spread and flanker men, the more you will confuse the defense.

The assignments on the opposite of this play, "48H," are the same for most of the men.   The big exception is that the quarterback should take one extra step before lateraling the ball out to the halfback.   Remember, however, that should your signal caller be left-handed, he would take three steps on "29H" and two on the opposite.

By putting the fullback out on a flanker on the opposite side we find that the ball carrier can advance further before running into mass opposition.   Frequently we will pass to the fullback when he is out in that flat, thus making it mandatory for the opponents to send a man out with him.   I sincerely believe that the duty of a flanker man cannot be overstressed, because he can render so many invaluable services to the team, especially when playing an opponent that has a definite pattern of defensive play.

"29H" AGAINST THE 5-3-2-1

The next defensive plan that we run into is a 5-3-2-1 set-up, which can be very troublesome unless the linebackers are drawn in by the faking of our backfield men.   As soon as the tackle sees this type of defense he calls "Right end out." This spreads the *right end* wide until he is about one yard outside the defensive end.   His duty then is to sprint past the onside linebacker, cut back, and drive him away from the hole. While the end is doing this, the *right tackle* executes a brush block on the opposing end before going downfield to engage the defensive halfback.

The *right guard* should charge through and remove the middle linebacker from the scene.   This opponent is usually fast and is in a good spot to see what is going on; therefore, he must be taken care of well.   The *center* finds a man directly on his head, so he stays with him for three full counts before releasing his block and joining the party.   Against this defense the *left guard* draws the assignment of blocking back on any opponents who recover in time to cause trouble.

The *left end* and *left tackle* should veer on downfield, getting themselves between the ball carrier and any potential

tacklers as soon as they possibly can.   The *backfield* performs
the same maneuvers as against a six-man line, with the quarterback working very hard to fake a good forward pass after
he laterals the ball.   The five-man line is always on the alert
for passes, and if the signal caller can force just one opponent
to believe that he is going to throw the ball, he may find that

"29H" against the 5-3-2-1:

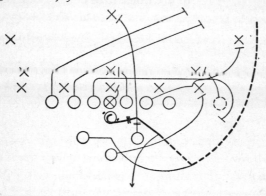

"48H" against the 5-3-2-1:

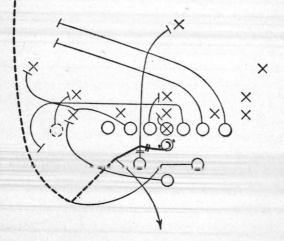

this opponent is the man who would have tackled the ball carrier.   If the right halfback is getting through the line and no one covers him, a pass over the center might crack the defense. Every play we have that ends with the number one man faking a pass can also be called as a pass from that formation. For example, the pass we have just described would be entitled "29H pass."

"29H" AGAINST A SEVEN-MAN LINE

Assuming that all assignments are carried out, "29H" can be especially potent against a seven-man line.   The importance of the right halfback's faking is doubled here, since perfect deception on his part will cause the defensive linemen to freeze in position.   If your number four back can render these seven men useless for two seconds, the number three back should be well on his way to a touchdown.   In the event that the opposing linemen are faked out, the offensive blockers will have the advantage in manpower as they sweep goalward. We usually find this defense to have the sole linebacker playing directly behind the center, and for that reason we have diagrammed the set-up in that manner on page 53.

Against such a defense the *right end* brush blocks the defensive end and sweeps outside the opposing halfback.   This will put him between that defender and our ball carrier.   The *right tackle* should block the guard into the hole where the right halfback will be coming through.   After making certain that this man is going in that direction, he should leave him so as to assist his teammate.   The *right guard* has the important assignment of removing the linebacker from the scene. All he has to do is to sprint right through the line and make contact with the enemy.   If he stops this man from moving over, the ball carrier should have much success.

The *center* moves with the ball and drives the man on his

head toward the sidelines with a shoulder block.   He should
give him a simple head fake and then start driving him just as
hard as he can.   Our *left guard* once again draws the assignment of blocking back to protect the ball carrier from being
trapped from behind.   The *left tackle* and *left end* should

"29H" against a seven-man line:

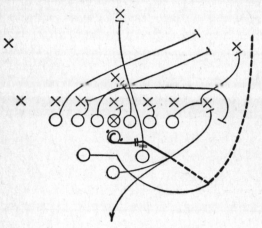

"48H" against a seven-man line:

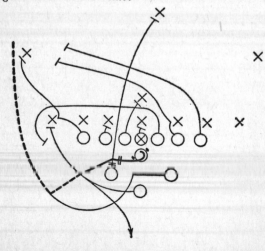

scuffle briefly with the men opposite them before going on downfield to work on the defensive backfield.

As a general rule, we do not run into the seven-man line very often when operating from the "T." However, it is usually employed when we near the goal line, and if there is plenty of room on our right, we may realize some good results if we run this play at the enemy. It must be run wide in order to give our blockers time to get into action. As mentioned before, it is not especially adaptable to scoring drives, but such a case as the above might catch the enemy napping.

"29H" AGAINST AN OVERSHIFTED SIX-MAN LINE

An overshifted six-man line necessitates a few changes in our offensive set-up. To overcome such a plan calls for a fast-stepping right tackle who can pull around fast enough to make the middle linebacker change his plans before he gets into the play. We have our *right end* perform the same duties as previously explained. The *right tackle* pulls high to screen the quarterback's maneuvers and moves around to hit the backer-up with a shoulder block. The *right guard* must move very fast to get at the defensive guard, since he has a very poor angle from which to work. A good head fake combined with quick action will put him in a position to do the job satisfactorily. The *center* works with the man on his head, while the remaining members of the team carry out the identical assignments that we gave against a seven-man line.

This play is styled to fit a "scatback" who shines the brightest in an open field. Such outstanding backs as Terry Brennan, Bob Livingstone, and Coy McGee have made many valuable yards for Notre Dame on "29H." It is a play that pays large dividends on good deception, which is an art that can be developed with hard work. We have been exceptionally fortunate in having such fine deceptive backs as Johnny

Lujack, George Ratterman, and Frank Tripucka. Not one of these lads was born with this talent, but continual hard work plus a willingness to learn developed them into top flight signal callers. Many times we would find these lads on the field before practice, each going over his spins and fakes, with the

"29H" against a six-man line overshifted to the right:

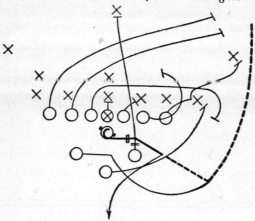

"48H" against a six-man line overshifted to the left:

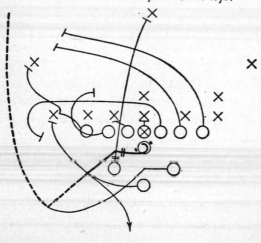

other two making critical suggestions and appraisals of the various movements.

HELPFUL HINTS FOR A SUCCESSFUL "29H"

For best results this play should be called soon after the quick-opener has worked successfully. At such a time the enemy will be extremely anxious to make contact with your right halfback. If this man executes a perfect fake, there is no reason why your left halfback should not have an opportunity to be on his way into the end zone. The left halfback should devote much practice to receiving this lateral. The more at ease he is catching the ball without turning his body, the smaller the chance that he will be detected immediately.

The ball carrier must assume that he will receive some downfield aid from his teammates. With this in mind, he should sweep wide, giving the blockers time to get over into position. He should not run ahead of his teammates, since they should delay to scuffle with the opponents. His job is to carry the mail over the goal line.

We believe that this play should be called rather early in the game in order that the quarterback will have a good idea of the comparative strength of the ends on defense. We had very little success with this play against Purdue in 1946 because their ends were extremely difficult to do business with. This was a great tribute to their Head Coach, and former great end, Stu Holcomb.

The quarterback should use any number of variations from this basic formation. If your left halfback can pass, have him do so from this play. We have never adopted this version to any extent, but coaches, such as Wally Butts of Georgia and Earl Blaik of Army, for example, used it to great advantage when they had Charley Trippi and Glenn Davis on their respective teams. If the quarterback will always remember to keep the plays simple, he will find that the men will not forget them under the pressure of battle.

A coach will find that this play is exceptionally pleasing to the audience, since the ball carrier is out where everyone can see him, and it is required that he do some fancy stepping to stay on his feet. After all, it is the fans who keep the turn-stiles clicking, so it is our job to give them a show that they will enjoy.

5

Mousetrap

THE TERM "mousetrap" has long been in use in the game of football. It is an old style of play that still gains yardage if executed properly. It will work particularly well against a very aggressive team. When the opponent is over-anxious to cross the line of scrimmage, we allow him to come ahead until we have a good angle on him for delayed blocking.

In our system we have the play set up as "21 trap" with the alternatives of it becoming "23" or "25." The change will be called at the line of scrimmage by the tackle when he sees how the defense is laid out. We change this play in the same manner as we do the "43"; that is, if the tackle sees the number one hole filled in, he calls "Up two," which makes the play a "23." We have never had any difficulty in changing the holes at the line of scrimmage; in fact, quite often it seems that the play works better when we are forced to do this. The main requirement on this play is that you have rugged, fast-moving tackles and guards who can pull out of the line without tipping off the play.

ASSIGNMENTS FOR THE MOUSETRAP

"21 TRAP" AGAINST A NORMAL SIX-MAN LINE

When facing a normal six-man line, as outlined on page 59, the *left end* should sprint through the line and make it his business to see that the safety man is in no position to halt the ball carrier when he comes into that zone.   He should not work too fast or the man may have time to recover.

We ask our *right tackle* to block the offside linebacker.   He should start through the line and cut over as soon as he has worked himself into a good blocking position.   He should be able to drive the enemy all the way to the sideline if necessary. If possible, he should see that the opponent moves in toward

"21 Trap" ("23 trap") against a normal six-man line:

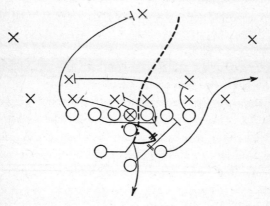

"40 Trap" ("42 trap") against a normal six-man line:

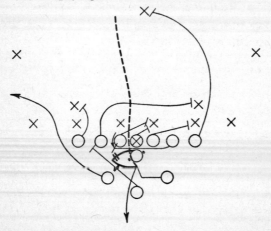

the line of scrimmage before he applies his shoulder block.

The *center* is the pressure blocker on the defensive right guard. He works with our *right guard,* who is the post blocker. These two men must double team this opponent, because he is in a most advantageous position to bottle up the offensive movement. Have these two men work together often. Ask them to establish a set of signals between themselves so that they can decide instantaneously which one is going to block high when his teammate goes in low. This is vitally important, since it is one of the few times in the "T" that we employ two-on-one blocking, and the lads are not too familiar with the plan.

The *left guard* should veer through the line and block the offside tackle away from the hole.

The *left tackle* is the man upon whom the success of the play depends. He must take one step back and face the sidelines. When cutting across he should hug the line of scrimmage, keeping low to avoid detection. As soon as the trapped guard steps across the line, the left tackle should start burying his shoulder in his opponent's midsection, driving him toward the sidelines. We tell our men to block very hard on this play, for the harder the man is hit, the more reluctant he will be to charge in on the following plays. When you have an opponent in this state, you will find that it is not too difficult to run plays through his hole. A man who naturally likes to crash is usually easy to block whenever he attempts to be cautious.

The *right end* should do business with the onside linebacker. We like to have him cut in away from the man before making the contact, since this makes it easier for him to block him away from the hole.

The *quarterback* has a big job to perform on this play. He does a great deal of moving around in the backfield prior to handing the ball off to the number two back. All of this maneuvering must be carefully screened to avoid detection.

We ask our signal caller to make a reverse pivot and take two steps at an angle to the scrimmage line of about forty-five degrees. This brings him into a position where he is met by the fullback, who is slanting off in the direction of our right end. A complete fake is executed at this point, with the quarterback pushing the ball right in until it touches the fullback's stomach. He then rides the ball back into his own stomach. At the same time he is shielding the activities by raising his left shoulder while he turns away from the line. As soon as the fullback is past, the quarterback takes two steps directly parallel with the line of scrimmage, which brings him to a point about two yards behind the center. Here he is met by the left halfback, who takes the ball on his right hip, grasps it, and moves it through the number one hole. Immediately after our quarterback releases the ball, we require him to fade back and fake a forward pass. Besides adding deception to the play, this maneuver puts our signal caller in a spot where he can analyze just what is going on in the front lines.

The *left halfback,* being the ball carrier, is the man we are most concerned with on this play. As soon as the ball is snapped he steps off, with his right foot, toward the right sideline. After taking two steps he commences to veer toward the number one hole. When he has taken two more steps he should be in a position to receive the ball from the quarterback. At this point his right leg will be back to avoid a fumble. As soon as the pigskin is in the pocket he must start to churn his legs and head for pay dirt. We like to have this back veer slightly to his right after he gets through the line. This allows the left end to work the opposing safety man over to the sidelines.

The *right halfback's* job is to make a solid fake at the opposing end and then cut parallel to the line on a forward pass decoy. This should bring their left halfback in close, thus allowing our ball carrier to run through his territory. Of course we have a "21 trap pass," which we occasionally throw to the right halfback if the opponent is not coming up fast enough to cover him.

The *fullback* is asked to work with the left tackle on the man being trapped. Frequently the tackle does not need the fullback's aid, in which case we ask the number three back to take care of the first man without a green shirt who comes across the line. All this happens, of course, after he has faked with the quarterback. The two little lines at the point where the fullback and quarterback meet indicate that they are executing a fake. Have your fullback practice doubling up fast in order to keep the pocket invisible and the enemy guessing.

"21 TRAP" AGAINST AN OVERSHIFTED SIX-MAN LINE

When we spot a six-man line overshifted to the side where we plan to run the play, we must make a few minor adjustments. As soon as the tackle notices this defense he will call "Up two," and the play will become a "23 trap." The obvious reason for this is that the defensive man playing opposite the center is a man who could stop the "21" play without too much difficulty. Moving the play over to the next hole makes it very simple for our center to double team with our right guard on the dangerous man. Another important change is that we ask our *left guard* to do the trapping rather than the *left tackle*. The reason for this change is that we feel the tackle is too far removed from his man to get there in time to block him correctly. Conversely, we feel that on "21 trap" the guard is too close to the man we want trapped, and his efforts might result in blocking the man before he gets across the line of scrimmage.

The *right end* is asked to sprint downfield for the purpose of removing the safety man from the path of our ball carrier. Have him allow enough time before he gets too far downfield for the left halfback to receive the ball from the quarterback.

The *right tackle* must move fast as he drives the center line-backer out and away from the hole. This man is a vital cog in the defensive set-up, and he must be well taken care of if the play is to succeed. As previously mentioned, the *right guard* and the *center* double team the man on the head of the center. In this maneuver we ask our center to act as the post blocker while the right guard becomes the pressure blocker.

"21 Trap" ("23 trap") against an overshifted six-man line:

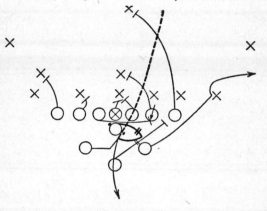

"40 Trap" ("42 trap") against an overshifted six-man line:

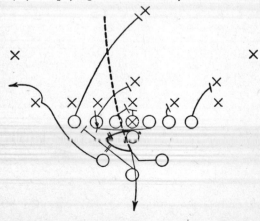

The *left guard* draws the big task on this play. He must step back and pivot toward the right sideline. He must sprint low and force his shoulder into the opponent before this man realizes he is being trapped. Our favorite phrase for this maneuver is, "Stay as low as you can as long as you can." Our *left tackle* scuffles with the man on his head until he is absolutely certain that it is safe for him to go downfield and block for the ball carrier. The *left end* should make certain that the offside linebacker will not cause us any trouble, and then he should join the touchdown crew.

The overshifting of the six-man line does not affect the duties of the *backfield* men, with the exception of the *fullback*. It becomes this man's job to see that the opposing left tackle is unable to get over in time to fill up the hole. This is one of the main reasons why we like to have a large fullback in our system. The ball carrying duties of a "T" fullback do not require that he be a big man, but oftentimes we ask our fullbacks to block the opposing ends and tackles, and for this reason they should be good-sized lads. Since installing this system at Notre Dame we have had comparatively small men in our number three spot, but what they lacked in size they all made up in determination and drive.

When running against this type of defense, it is especially important to check on how well your right halfback is guarded as he goes out on a pass decoy. Ordinarily such a defense is vulnerable to passes in his direction.

"21 TRAP" AGAINST THE 5-3-2-1

A 5-3-2-1 defense should permit remarkable results with this play, assuming your right halfback can draw the defensive left halfback over to the sidelines. Once again it is required for best results that the play be moved over to make it a "23 trap." However, you may find that many times an opponent will be in a five-man line but spaced in such a manner that "21" would be the best play to call. This is one good reason why we like to have our men call the assignments by location of the enemy rather than by the name of the defense. Some coaches prefer to have one set offense for a five-man line, another for a six, and so on. However, experience has taught us that our method is more elastic.

On this play we have our *right end* charge straight through

"21 Trap" ("23 trap") against the 5-3-2-1:

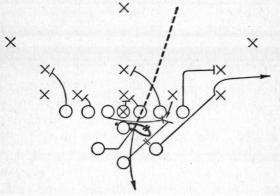

"40 Trap" ("42 trap") against the 5-3-2-1:

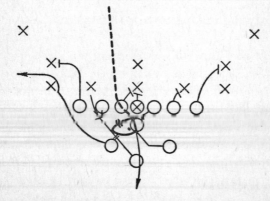

before veering into the onside linebacker.   In this manner he can then maneuver the opponent all the way to the bench if desired.   This opponent may even be drawn out of the play by the decoy back, in which case our end heads right on downfield to help out with the blocking in that sector.   The *right tackle's* assignment is the same as against an overshifted six-man line; that is, to remove the middle linebacker as soon as possible.

Once again we have our *center* double team with our *right guard* on taking the man playing opposite the snapper-back. Our *left guard* has more ground to cover when we run up against such a defense.   The man to be "trapped" will be coming through on the outer side of our tackle, rather than between the guard and tackle.   In view of this, we ask our guard to move that much faster.   If the blocking guard will keep as close to the line as possible, he will find that the fullback will come up fast and give him some assistance with the enemy lineman.   Instruct your guards that they must not allow the defensive man to knife in front of them.   The remaining members of the team will follow through with their original assignments, with the fullback moving up fast to aid the guard.   We use a flanker quite often on this plan because it tends to break up the enemy strategy.

"21 TRAP" AGAINST A SEVEN-MAN LINE

A seven-man line, with its compactness, presents some different problems to the man calling the blocking assignments. The *right end* will follow the same pattern as he did against an overshifted line, when he moved downfield to tangle with the enemy safety man.   The *right tackle* has a very important job to do on this play, since the man to be trapped is playing directly opposite him.   We ask him to brush block the opposing lineman just enough to make certain that the opponent will have to go to our man's right in order to get into our backfield. We do not want our tackle to stop the man from coming in, but we do want him to come in through the hole where our trapping guard will be expecting him. If the tackle properly executes this maneuver, the man will be in an excellent position to be blocked as he comes through the line.

Again we ask our *right guard* to act as the pressure blocker

"21 Trap" ("23 trap") against a seven-man line:

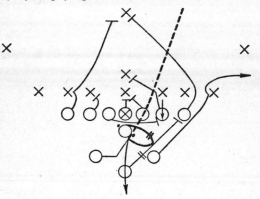

"40 Trap" ("42 trap") against a seven-man line:

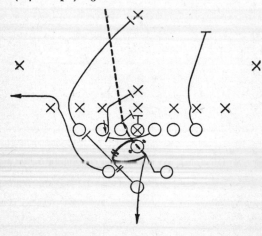

as he coöperates with the *center* on the first man to the left of the hole.   The *left tackle* and the *left end* should spend three full counts with the men across the line before they move on downfield to assist the ball carrier.   The *backfield* men fulfill their same duties with the exception of the *fullback*, who takes out the first opponent across the line.

"23 TRAP"

Notice that when the play moves up to a "23 trap" the ball carrier has that much further to move after he takes the ball.   This is a play in which the hours spent on quarterbacking will prove fruitful.   If just one of the opponents is looking at the quarterback when the ball carrier goes by, it may very well be the difference between a one-yard gain and a touchdown.   Overemphasize the fact that you want all of the fakes exaggerated.   Whenever your backfield men are not taking part in the actual practice, have them work with a quarterback on the various exchanges.   They can never get to be too good at this part of the game.   It should improve a little bit each day.   (See photos of this play following page 132.)

HINTS THAT SHOULD HELP TO BUILD
A BETTER MOUSETRAP

We ask our guard and center to analyze the situation thoroughly before they decide which man will be the post blocker while the other applies the pressure.   Here we have outlined all plays with the center being the post man, but they might run into a defensive set-up that could best be counteracted by the opposite assignments.

The way we help our men to remember who is to do the trapping is to tell them we want the offside tackle to do all the trapping on a one or zero trap, whereas the offside guard should take over this assignment on a three, five, two, or four trap. For most accurate timing we have found that the designated men can do the best job under the above conditions.

Without fear of appearing overly repetitious, we want to stress again the importance of good faking. If the men will learn this, they will soon find that it makes the assignments much easier for all hands. We would rather see two men following our right halfback out into the flat than to see the same two men blocked out of the play. If they are blocked out, they will react faster because they know where the play is going, but if they are faked out they are lost temporarily. One of the greatest signs of a good faking job is when your quarterback is tackled as he fades back to pass without the ball. A quarterback without sufficient fortitude is likely to tip his hand, but the great ones will lead the enemy all the way back with them.

6

Fullback Lateral

THIS IS A PLAY which we find works exceptionally well against a team that has crashing ends. The delayed maneuvers of this play cause the fast-rushing ends to converge on the quarterback. Such action leaves the end spots vulnerable for a sweep when the ball is lateraled out to the fullback. Notre Dame had an amazing degree of success with this play against Army in 1947. The first time our fullback, Mike Swistowicz, carried the ball on this play he gained thirty-five yards. We send the right halfback in motion on this play for the purpose of disconcerting the enemy. As a general rule, when a man goes in motion he is closely tagged by an opponent, which makes it quite easy for him to gain a fairly good blocking angle on the enemy, before the latter realizes that our man is not to receive a pass.

ASSIGNMENTS FOR THE FULLBACK LATERAL

FULLBACK LATERAL AGAINST A NORMAL SIX-MAN LINE

When facing a normal six-man line, we ask our *right end* to step out fast and brush block the enemy end before moving downfield to act as a convoy for the fullback. Our *right tackle* has the important task of stopping the onside linebacker before he can interfere with the play. This man will cause a great deal of trouble if he is not blocked out toward the left sideline. Our *right guard* is requested to keep the man

70

on his head occupied for three full counts **prior to** releasing
his block and joining the downfield crew.

We call upon our *center* to block back on this play, which
means when he gets outside of the end he should turn in the
direction from which the ball carrier came.   That is his area,

"39 Lateral, fake 23 trap" against a normal six-man line:

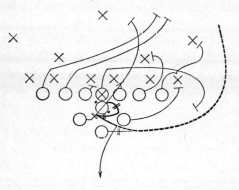

"38 Lateral, fake 42 trap" against a normal six-man line:

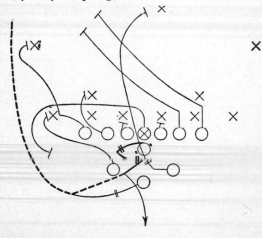

and he is instructed not to allow any potential tacklers to pass through it.   This assignment carries added importance on this play because, as a general rule, coaches will find that their full-backs are a little slower than the rest of the backs; therefore, there is a greater possibility of them being pulled down from behind.

The *left guard* and *left end* should spend three full counts scuffling with the men playing opposite them.   After they have them off balance they should release their blocks and sprint on downfield.   The *left tackle* has an open field in front of him, so we ask him to be the first man into the enemy secondary.

The name we have given to this play is "39 lateral, fake 23 trap."   Therefore, our backs perform the same duties for which they are called upon when executing a trap play.   Our *quarterback* makes a reverse pivot, takes two steps, and *fakes* a lateral out to the fullback.   This should be a very poor fake by both parties, because we want the opponents to know that the fullback does not get the ball.   Our fullback comes up tall and puts his hands up in front of his face to show everyone that he does not have the pigskin.   This maneuver is indicated by the first little set of lines in the paths of these two men. On the next movement, the quarterback turns toward the opposite sideline, takes two steps, and fakes a perfect "23 trap" with our number two back.   The better this fake, the more yards the play will realize.   As soon as the left halfback has gone, the signal caller turns about and steps in the direction of the fullback.   It is now that he should pass the ball out to the fullback.   When the lateral is actually coming to the fullback, he should remember to do all of the things outlined for our halfbacks on play number "29H."   He should "look" the ball all the way into his hands before glancing about for any potential tacklers.   If the *left halfback* is tackled on this play, we feel that he is giving 100 percent to see the ball moving in the proper direction.   The *right halfback's* duties are to see that the defensive end does not move out into the flat and slow down the play. He must make that man cut inside of him so that if he does recover, the center will be there to prevent him from catching up with the ball carrier.

The *fullback* will find that if he fakes very poorly at the outset, he later will be in a position to move the ball quite some distance before being molested. A good method is to have him act as if he were to catch a basketball.

Coaches will find that if their linemen are aggressive, they will have sufficient time to get over into blocking position before the fullback is in need of their talents. The time elapsed while the backs are carrying out their respective assignments is ample to allow the linemen to transact their business at the line and move over into the fracas. When you have two good fullbacks, suggest to the quarterback that he employ this attack when the shiftier man is in the ball game.

FULLBACK LATERAL AGAINST AN OVERSHIFTED
SIX-MAN LINE

A six-man line that is overshifted to the right gives us a bit more room to operate this play, if we can get the jump on the onside linemen. The *right end* performs the same job as against the normal six-man line while the *right tackle* has to do some fast stepping. We want him to circle the defensive tackle, bump him with a solid shoulder, but not waste any time on him. As soon as he is certain that this man will have to go through to his left, he steps forward and makes it his business to see that the middle linebacker does not move over into the play. He should not go after this man, but if the man starts to sift over, we want him stopped cold.

We ask our *right guard* to drive the defensive guard in toward the center of the line. The *center* has a man on his head, and we ask him to stick with him until the play is far down the field.   Against this defense the *left guard* draws the assignment of blocking back on an automatic exchange from the center.   The two remaining linemen are free to sprint immediately into the area covered by the opposing left halfback. These men should be there in plenty of time for the fullback to make use of their blocking talent.   The *backfield* men

"39 Lateral, fake 23 trap" against an overshifted six-man line:

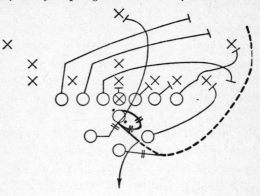

"38 Lateral, fake 42 trap" against an overshifted six-man line:

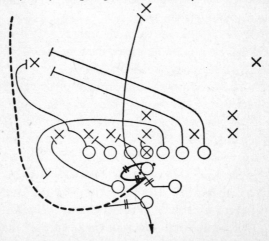

carry out the same maneuvers as against all types of defenses, but we do ask our *right halfback* to move out a little faster than usual, in view of the fact that the defensive end will be spread out just a few feet wider when the enemy is employing an overshifted six-man line.

FULLBACK LATERAL AGAINST THE 5-3-2-1

Perfect faking pays large dividends when this play is called against a five-man line.   What we desire to do is to draw the linebackers up into the holes, supposedly to stop the trap play that is being faked.   If such a maneuver can be brought about, the fullback will find it much easier to go around the end.

The *right end* and *right tackle* draw the same assignments as against an overshifted six, with the exception of the place we expect the onside linebacker to be stationed.   Since he is out nearer to the playing area, we ask our tackle to work hard to assure that this man does not get any farther away from the line of scrimmage than he is when the play begins to unfold. The element of surprise should confuse him long enough for the tackle to make his contact.

The *right guard* charges through and takes the middle linebacker, while the remaining three men perform the identical tasks for which they were called upon against the last defensive plan.   Have these men move fast and vary their methods of going downfield.   This will keep the defensive backfield guessing as to just what type of play to expect.   These men should work together often; ask them to develop a code system for informing each other as to who will block the first man into their zone.   Teamwork plays a most important part in downfield blocking.   All too often we see three or four men downfield who waste their talents by converging on the same opponent.   One man can block in the open field if he lets the potential tackler come to him.   He should always remember that the enemy must come to him if he expects to make the tackle.

"39 Lateral, fake 23 trap" against the 5-3-2-1:

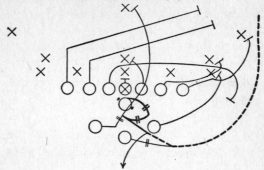

"38 Lateral, fake 42 trap" against the 5-3-2-1:

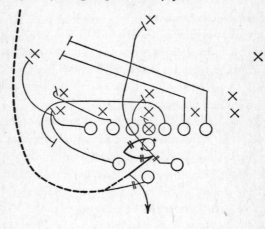

FULLBACK LATERAL AGAINST A SEVEN-MAN LINE

The seven-man line permits man-for-man blocking across the line and makes it mandatory that our offside linemen spend two seconds with the men opposing them before releasing. This is necessary because if the opponents see that our linemen are sprinting right out, they will be able to diagnose the play and also will be in a position to stop our men from getting out in time to be of service as downfield blockers.

We use almost the same tactics as were employed when facing a normal six-man line; that is, the *right end* out and down after brushing shoulders with the defensive end. The *right*

"39 Lateral, fake 23 trap" against a seven-man line:

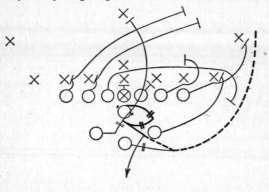

"38 Lateral, fake 42 trap" against a seven-man line:

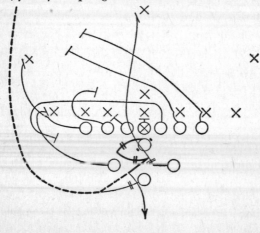

tackle takes care of the only linebacker. Since, in this instance, this man is playing opposite the center, the tackle should let him come to him. If he is pulled into the line by the fake, the tackle should forget about him and go looking for a man to block. Here we have a man on the *center's* head, so he and our left guard exchange assignments. This maneuver sends the left guard out and around to block back at the line of scrimmage. The *offside tackle* and *end* should put good, solid shoulder blocks on their opponents before they take off toward the end zone. A good method is to bump the man once, then give him a good head fake—which should throw him out of position, and leave him in that state.

You will notice that we have not assigned a man to block out the defending left tackle on any one of these plans. This is because we have found that this man is instinctively drawn in by the faking; by the time he recovers, the only way he can cause trouble is by cutting back through the territory that is being guarded by our center or left guard. We do not like to waste one second with a man who is not going to do us any harm.

Another reason for allowing this man to be free is that he is the man who would be trapped on our "23 trap" play. Permitting him to come in of his own accord makes it look as if we plan to trap him. Under such conditions, one of two things usually occurs: First, he will sense the trap and hold back until the play is out of his reach, or second, he will try to reach the quarterback before he releases the ball, thus taking himself out of the play altogether.

SUGGESTIONS ON "39 LATERAL"

Try to run this play in the same series in which you use the trap play. One will help the other immeasurably. A helpful innovation to this play will be realized if you have a fullback who can pass. Just an average passer will suffice. We find that many times when the two ends arrive downfield they

are in an ideal position to receive a pass.   Such a pass play will
keep the defensive backs from moving up too soon when you
run the play again.

Still another pass may be worked by having the quarterback keep the ball throughout and fade back to pass.   In order for this play to be carried out successfully, your quarterback must have much poise and confidence, since the natural
tendency is for him to hurry through his fakes, thus making
them of no value whatsoever.

As with the others described, this play can be run to either
side of the line.   Frequently you will notice that your fullback runs harder to his left, in which case it would be better to
make the play a "38" instead of a "39."   For best results, run
the play toward the wide-open side of the field, for if given
enough room, the ball carrier can usually make his way.

It was on this very play that John Panelli became one
of the nation's leading ground gainers during the 1948 season.   Against Nebraska, Panelli ran seventy-three yards for a
touchdown on such a maneuver, and on the opening play of
our game with Iowa the same young man carried the ball for
thirty-nine yards and six points on the "fullback lateral."   In
fact, we have been informed that every man who scouted us
during 1948 gave the report that this play was the most dangerous part of our entire attack.

7

End Around

THIS PLAY, which we have entitled "67F," was added to our system in the spring of 1947. Since we were faring successfully in the early part of that season, we did not use it in any of our games until we played Army. Naturally we feared the West Pointers a great deal, and we felt that it would be prudent on our part to save any exceptionally good plays until that contest. In this instance our strategy paid off; James Martin, our left end, was the leading ground gainer from the line of scrimmage on that Saturday afternoon. On two occasions Jim lost his footing after he had broken away from the line of scrimmage; otherwise we might have had two touchdowns.

As the name describes the play, it means the number six man, our left end, going through the number seven hole, which is off the right hip of our right end. The "F" indicates that our fullback contributes a fake. This play works equally well from either end. It so happened that in 1947 Jim Martin, at 200 pounds, made a faster ball carrier than did Leon Hart, who was our number one right end, at 220. This play will work exceptionally well on a day that your fullback is meeting with success in going through the line. A good fake by the fullback makes the play more deceptive when the quarterback turns his back completely on the opponents, thus making it exceedingly difficult for them to follow the ball.

As a general rule we post the left halfback out on a flanker on this play, with the hope that one of the defensive men will go out to cover him and leave enough room for our left end to cut up the field after he has gone through the number seven hole. We installed a blocking set-up for this play that is a little bit more difficult than usual, but we feel that it is necessary if we are to get the maximum out of such a maneuver.

ASSIGNMENTS FOR THE END AROUND

"67F" AGAINST A NORMAL SIX-MAN LINE

The *right end* is asked to make certain that the defensive tackle is driven away from the hole. He must get to this man fairly fast because a big man must be moved early in order to assure the left end a hole through which he may carry the mail. A head fake to the inside before attacking from the outside should do the trick.

The *right tackle* should have about the same angle on the defensive guard. His task looks comparatively easy, but he must remember that if he lets up for one split second, the entire play may be stopped. He should block the man in toward the center being careful that the guard does not pivot around him.

The *right guard's* duty is to pull out, go behind the tackle and end, and block the onside linebacker. This is the most important assignment, since that man is standing directly in the path that our ball carrier will be taking. We ask the guard to keep low and hug the line of scrimmage when he pulls. He should run outside of the linebacker and drive him in toward the middle of the gridiron. Have him scuffle with this man for some time, because it will require a few seconds for your end to get around to that spot.

Our *center* takes one step forward before cutting sharply to his left to block the offside guard. Once again he has a fairly good angle and should not have too much trouble if he starts to move as soon as he feels the ball leave his hand.

Our *left guard* has to move fast in order to carry out his assignment in time. We ask him to pull, staying between the quarterback and the line of scrimmage. He must follow the general rules for pulling linemen, and when he gets to the

"67F" against a normal six-man line:

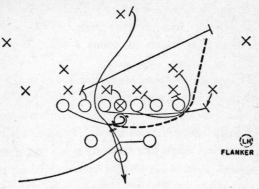

"56F" against a normal six-man line:

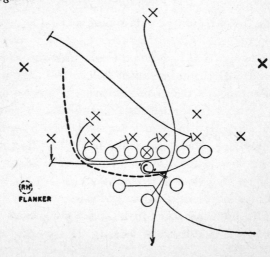

right side of the line, he should be on the lookout for the defensive end, who probably will be coming through. Ask the guard to let this man come across the line before hitting him with a shoulder block. If the offensive man keeps low while pulling, he should have a terrific advantage over his opponent, because, as a general rule, the end does not run up against a block from such an angle.

We like our *left tackle* to scuffle with the opposing tackle long enough to give the impression that our fullback is really intending to come through that hole. After about three full counts he should release his block and see of what use he can make himself on down the field.

The ball-carrying *left end* should take one full step backward and then step off toward the right sideline. By the time he reaches the quarterback he should be approximately two yards behind the line of scrimmage. The end must spend a great deal of time in practice figuring out exactly how many steps he must take in order that he will be stepping off with his right foot when he reaches the signal caller. If he does this, it will allow him to take the ball on his left side as his left leg is going back—thus making it more difficult to fumble. As soon as he gets the ball he should begin to size up the situation as it is unfolding. He should watch his left guard and edge into a spot where this man's block will do the most good. While the guard bumps the man out, the end should cut in through the number seven hole. Once through the hole, the end should fade over toward the right sideline if possible. Frequently the defensive left halfback makes this an impossibility, but if he has been removed, the end can work his way over there and make use of the linemen who have released their blocks and are trying to be of assistance.

The *quarterback* does a reverse pivot and takes one full step over to make the fake to the fullback. He should make it a good fake and then wait for the end to come around. Do not let him get in the habit of looking for the end. We ask our quarterbacks to take a look at the scoreboard at this time in order to prevent them from being tempted to watch to see if the end is going to make it. When the end arrives, the quarterback hands the ball to him in the same manner as the pass-off was made on the number "43" play. After the hand off, the quarterback should fade back and fake a forward pass, still looking in the direction of the scoreboard. This is important—the hand off to the end may go unnoticed if the quarterback does not keep looking after him.

As previously mentioned, we station the *left halfback* out on a flanker position on this play. By putting him out to the right and having the *right halfback* "fly" out to the left, we have spread the defenders behind the line on both sides, thus leaving a good opening up through the middle. The right halfback should take about three steps over before beginning to "belly" back. He should sweep wide and keep his eyes open to see who follows him. If he is left alone, he might make an excellent target for a forward pass a few plays later. Whenever such a play is stopped "cold," try to find out why. Usually it is because the opponent is leaving some spot unguarded in order to double his guard on the hole side. When this occurs, run the same basic play, but have the quarterback either hand off the ball to the fullback or take it back and pass out to one of the halfbacks.

As soon as the ball is snapped the *fullback* should step out in the direction of the number two hole. When making the fake with the quarterback, have the fullback double up and charge rapidly into the line.

When we first installed this play in our system we had our right guard blocking the defensive end rather than our left guard. After running the play a few times, we found that the right guard was getting there too soon while the left guard had to work very fast in order to remove the linebacker from the scene. Switching the assignments of these two men gave them plenty of time to carry out their individual blocks.

After the play has been run a number of times in practice, you will notice that the left end is able to cut back on a forty-five degree angle rather than having to make a sharp pivot, as we like to have them do when starting out. Teach your ends some of the tricks that help backfield men, such as, dropping the shoulder, stiff-arming, and side-stepping. There is no reason why your ends cannot be as dangerous when they have the ball as are your backs.

"67F" AGAINST AN OVERSHIFTED SIX-MAN LINE

When "67F" is called upon to face a six-man line that is overshifted to the right, we do not have too many changes in the original blocking assignments. We ask our *right end* and *right tackle* to follow the same instructions they were given to combat a normal six-man line; that is, to block the man opposite them in toward the center of the line.

The *right guard* has the big change on this play, since the man he was to block in the original set-up has moved over behind the center. Now, instead of pulling, we ask him to sprint right through and make sure that the man backing up the line does not shift over toward the number seven hole. There is a possibility that this opponent may be taken out of the play by the fullback's fake, and, if so, do not allow the guard to waste any time with him. With a man playing directly on the head of the *center,* it would be most advantageous if the latter were to block him away from the hole side. We ask the center to do this unless it would be easier for him to exchange assignments with the right guard.

The *left guard* is the big gun on this play because he has to move over fast and remove the defensive end from the ball carrier's line of fire. On this play he has the same job as he did against the normal six-man line, except that he will find that the left end plays wider and may have a tendency to veer in rather than coming in in a straight line. If such is the case, it will be necessary for our guard to get himself between the end and the line of scrimmage and make certain that this man does not knife through. The *left tackle* will be used primarily as a downfield blocker. First, he should spend a couple of seconds making certain that no one on his side of the line is pulling out and circling behind the line.

The backfield men carry out the identical assignments,

"67F" against a six-man line overshifted to the right:

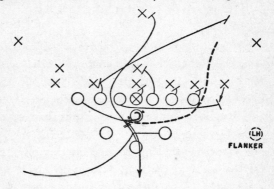

"56F" against a six-man line overshifted to the left:

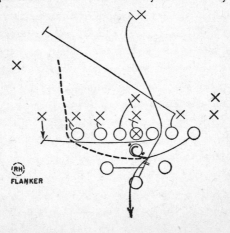

with the *fullback* going through to eliminate the safety man. However, we would much rather see the fullback tackled at the line of scrimmage, since this would take more men out of the play and prove to us that our players' main interest is to see that the ball is advanced, regardless of who is carrying it.

"67F" AGAINST THE 5-3-2-1

A 5-3-2-1 defense brings about a few more changes in our strategy for "67F." The *right end* still has the same assignment of blocking the defensive tackle in toward the center of the line. The *right tackle* has a much more important maneuver on this play, since we ask him to go through the line and remove the middle backer-up from the danger zone. He should make certain that when contact is initiated he is in an advantageous position to block the linebacker away from the hole side.

Our *right guard* goes back to his original task of pulling and running in front of the ball carrier to block the onside backer-up. He must get there fast, since this man is directly in the path and must be removed if the play is to succeed.

The *center* has a man on his head and it is his duty to see that this man is driven away from the hole. He should step out with his right foot and then bury his shoulder deep in the enemy lineman.

Once again the *left guard* is leading the parade around the right end. His man, the left end, may be playing just a little wider in this set-up, in which case the guard must run a bit faster if he is to finish the work before the ball carrier gets there. The *left tackle* makes a good head fake as he brushes past the offside tackle. As soon as this man is off balance our tackle heads down to work with the fullback on the enemy safety man.

The *backfield* men perform the same chores, although against this defense the fullback has a better chance of going through the line to get the safety man.   However, we would still prefer to see him tackled.

"67F" *against the* 5-3-2-1:

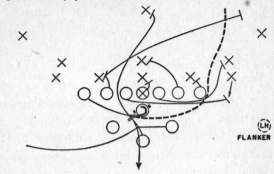

"56F" *against the* 5-3-2-1:

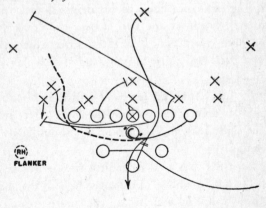

"67F" AGAINST A SEVEN-MAN LINE

When this play is called and the defense lines up in a seven-man line, we must be positive that every man carries out his assignment; otherwise the enemy may break through before the play is started. The *right end* is in a position to get a fairly good angle on the defensive tackle. He should charge directly at this man and stick with him until the ball carrier is free. The *right tackle's* angle is about the same, and he applies the same type of block on the opposing guard. We call upon our *right guard* to go through and make certain that the linebacker is unable to pull behind and stop the end

"67F" against a seven-man line:

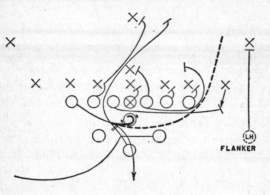

"56F" against a seven-man line:

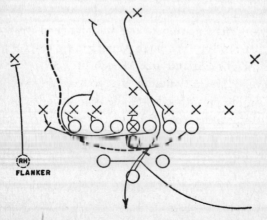

as he comes through the number seven hole.   The *pivot man* is still working with a man directly opposite him, and we want that man driven away from the hole.

The *left guard* is still the convoy man and he pulls low behind the line to block the end out and back from the hole. The *left tackle* should spend about two full counts with the man opposite him before releasing and heading for the safety man.

We expect our *fullback* to be tackled on this play.   The defensive right guard is free and it is through his hole that we have our fullback run.   It pleases us when this man does tackle the fullback, since there is a possibility that the former could get through before the end receives the ball from the quarterback.   If the fullback notices that the opponent is coming in for the ball carrier, then he should hit him with a good solid shoulder block.   This will give the end time to get away.   By using both the flanker and the man-in-motion, we try to force the enemy to loosen up their defense, thus allowing our end to cut into a fairly open field.

HINTS ON SWEEPING THE END

We like to have our ends spend some time practicing with the backs, so they will develop the necessary finesse in receiving the ball from the quarterback.   Whenever they hear us giving any information to our ball carriers, we want them to listen carefully.   As such outstanding players as Leon Hart, Bill Wightkin, and Jim Martin proved to us, your ends can be every bit as valuable to you as a good halfback. This is a simple play that takes the opponent by surprise.   It is a good thing to let your ends work out with your fullbacks when they are practicing the shoulder drop.   This little maneuver works best when used by a big man, and as a general rule the ends are larger than the backs.

Run this play frequently during a game, since it will give

your backs a rest and will keep the linemen more alert throughout the contest. Practice running the sweep from both ends; you may be hemmed in too close to a sideline for it to work properly as "67F" when all other conditions point to a successful play.

8

Scoring Threat

PLAY "27F" and its opposite "46F" have been top flight scoring threats in the Notre Dame "T" offense ever since its inception in 1942. They are plays that demand a great deal of teamwork since each member of the backfield has an important duty to perform. These have been our number one touchdown plays, and were our strongest weapon against the Army in 1947, when Bob Livingstone scored one touchdown and Terry Brennan another on the simple "27F." Neither of the above mentioned young men had a hand laid on him as he went across the goal line. Number "27F" is another play, like "43," that many coaches are likely to abandon because of its simplicity, but we feel that *because* of this simplicity it is a great play. If you ever run up against a team that will stop this maneuver continually, then you are facing a great defensive unit.

ASSIGNMENTS FOR "27F"

"27F" AGAINST A NORMAL SIX-MAN LINE

We find that because this play is so basic the blocking assignments do not change much with the defense. When facing a normal six-man line, we have our *right end* block the defensive tackle in toward the center and back in the direction of the line of scrimmage. The end should move fast, because this is a very important assignment. The *right tackle* has a good angle on the defensive guard, so we like to have him take one step across the line and then cut over and into the guard. As soon as the contact is made he should start taking short, digging steps.

The *right guard* draws the important blocking job on this play, and that is to pull out to his right and hug the line of scrimmage. As soon as he sees the opposing end step across the line he should head for him with the express purpose of burying his shoulder deep in the enemy's midsection. He should keep his eyes on his opponent's waist; a good end might

"27F" against a normal six-man line:

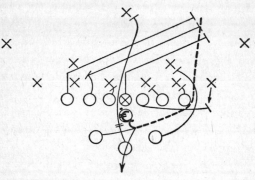

"46F" against a normal six-man line:

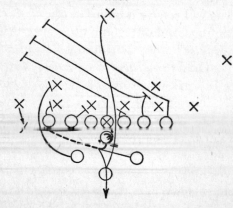

fake our man out of position if he is looking at the end's head or feet. We have our *center* sprint across the line for about three yards and then veer over into the vicinity where the defensive left halfback is stationed. The *left guard* should scuffle with the man on his head for at least three full counts before heading in the direction of the ball carrier. As previously mentioned, this play is often used very close to the goal line, in which case we ask our linemen to stick with their target until the play is completed.

The *left tackle* should charge over to the offside linebacker and make contact with him for about two full counts. As soon as this man has been forced off balance, the tackle should leave him and slant over toward the right sideline. The *left end* should cut behind the offside linebacker and move himself into a position that will be between the safety man and our ball carrier. If possible, he should allow the offside backer-up to think that he is coming for him, and this will make things that much easier for your own left tackle.

In the backfield we have the *quarterback* stop in the middle of his reverse pivot to fake handing off the ball to the fullback as he comes heading into the number zero hole. After making a good hard fake to this runner, the quarterback completes the pivot and takes one step out with the right foot. As his right leg is going out, he hands the ball off to the left halfback, who will receive it on his left hip. Be careful when first teaching this hand off; you must realize that the angle is quite a bit different from that brought about when carrying out a "43." The *left halfback* should delay for a split second to allow the fullback to get out of the way. Have the number two back start off with his right foot and run at a forty-five degree angle to the line of scrimmage. On his third step he should be in a position to receive the ball from the quarterback. At this time his right foot should be forward and his left back, forming a pocket at his left hip bone. The two hands should be down near this point ready to receive the ball as the quarterback feeds it in. He grasps the ball and keeps veering at approximately the same angle until he arrives at the number seven hole. Once through the hole he is on his own, although we believe that for best results the back should keep on going straight down the field. Naturally, existing circumstances may cause the ball carrier to run in a different direction every time. If the play is called at a point very close to the enemy goal line, we have noticed that our backs cut sharply to their left as soon as they are through the line. This method takes them away from the defensive left half-back, of course, and they are into pay territory before the safety man can come up to make the tackle. This maneuver will vary with the individual—so long as the scoreboard registers six points we will not complain. The moment the ball is snapped, the *fullback* heads for the left hip of the center. After making a good fake with the quarterback, he should double up and smash into the line as if he really had some place to go.

The *right halfback* has a very important job to do on this play. As soon as the play begins he should sprint through the number seven hole, circling around behind the line to come up on the outside linebacker from the most advantageous angle possible. He should give this man a good head fake toward the goal line and then drive him back toward the line of scrimmage. Ask him to make use of the head fake because generally he will find that this man outweighs him.

"27F" AGAINST AN OVERSHIFTED SIX-MAN LINE

When "27F" is called and the defense lines up in a six-man line that is overshifted to the right, we have virtually the same blocking assignments already described for each member of our team. The men on the right side of the line will find that their targets are lined up a little closer to them. This may prove advantageous, but if not, our linemen should be able to assume a good angle as they get into their stance when the quarterback calls "Down."

The main difference on this play is that the man to be blocked by the *right halfback* is stationed directly behind the center.　When the number four back gets through the line, rather than going over after this linebacker, he should see if anyone is seeping into the area that he is guarding.　If it is a close yardage situation, the safety man might sense the play

"27F" against a six-man line overshifted to the right:

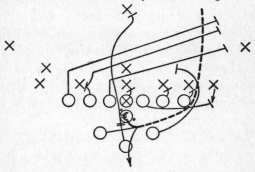

"46F" against a six-man line overshifted to the left:

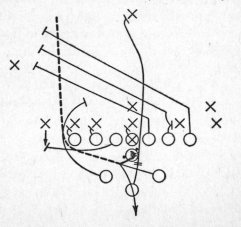

and come up fast. In this case the right halfback should be sure that this man is well taken care of. A player should never chase a man who is outside of the danger zone.

As the *quarterback* fades back to pass, he should pay special attention to the coverage given our left end and right half-back while they go about their blocking duties. These two men are potential pass receivers who are operating in zones that are not overcrowded with defensive men. Since this is the case, it might be an opportune moment to cross up the defense by throwing a forward pass to one of the above lads.

This play works very well to either side of the line, but when facing a six-man line that is overshifted to the right, we find that the "27F" bears more fruit than the "46F." Our thinking on this is that our ball carrier will run into much less trouble once he gets through the line on the right side of the field.

"27F" AGAINST THE 5-3-2-1

A 5-3-2-1 defense presents a few different problems, which, if coped with correctly, should send your ball carrier into an open field. We ask our *right end* to take one full step straight ahead as soon as the ball is snapped. He then should pivot on a ninety-degree angle and charge toward the defensive end. By this time the opponent should be across the line and our man should be able to drive him completely out of the play. This is a fast-moving play, therefore our end must get to work immediately after he takes that one step toward the enemy goal line.

The *left tackle* will have to move out to his right a little before he can start to block on the opposing tackle. He should do this rapidly before the enemy can sense which way our left end is going. This time the *right guard* goes directly through and forces his shoulder into the middle backer-up.

If blocked early, this man should not prove troublesome to our ball carrier. The *center* has a man directly on his head and he should be sure that this man is driven out to the opposite sideline. The entire left side of the line should move downfield to assist the ball carrier. We ask these offside linemen to stay about the same distance apart as they were when the play lined up; that is, they should step out together and keep the spacing the same all the way down the field. The

"*27F*" *against the* 5-3-2-1:

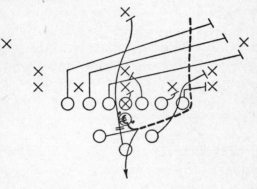

"*46F*" *against the* 5-3-2-1:

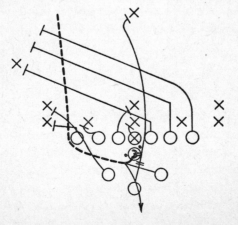

reason for this is that if the men run too close together they get in each other's way, and the blocks become ineffective. Or if they begin to spread apart, they will find that the opponents are able to sift through their open ranks. It is much easier to maintain the same spacing, and much more profitable for all concerned.

Once again the only change in the backfield activity concerns the *right halfback*. Against this type of defense we have him run inside of our right end and cut out to remove the onside linebacker. This defensive man should be driven out and away from the hole. Even though he is the smaller player, our right halfback should be able to scuffle with this man long enough to render him helpless. If he gets the jump on the man, he should have no trouble. In 1947 none of our halfbacks weighed more than 175 pounds, but they were able to block hard enough and long enough to make this play a success. In fact, at the time Bob Livingstone scored in the Army contest, Larry Coutre, who weighs 155 pounds, was playing at right halfback. Size does not matter a great deal in such a case if the man possesses that burning desire to see his teammate in the end zone. In fact, we have found at Notre Dame that small backs are particularly effective blockers. Of course it is essential that you have big linemen to open the holes, but large size is not one of the important requirements in a backfield man.

"27F" AGAINST A SEVEN-MAN LINE

The final defense against which we have set up "27F" is the seven-man line. The blocking assignments are the same as against a six-man line. However, in this instance we do ask our offside linemen to spend a few seconds with the linemen opposite them, for two very good reasons. First, it would "tip off" the play too soon if our linemen were to "fly" out without making any attempt to stop the enemy.   Second, if our linemen do not get the jump on the opponents they may find that these men will knock them off balance and prevent them from arriving down the field in time to be of any use to the ball carrier.   In this instance, as in all others, we let our center and offside guard decide who is going to take the man playing opposite them.

"27F" against a seven-man line:

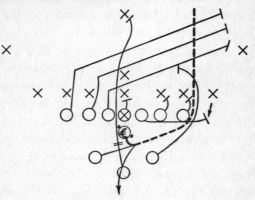

"46F" against a seven-man line:

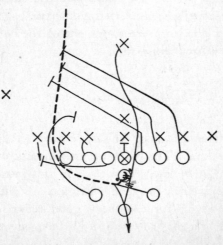

SUGGESTIONS TO GO WITH "27F"

This play is adaptable to any place on the gridiron. We have always liked to use it down in pay territory because it combines the elements of speed and deception to a high degree. This does not mean that it should not be used in the open field; in fact, we have used it with much success from all parts of the field. Early in the game, if you notice that the opponent is geared to slow down your quick-opener and is also very cautious when following your deceptive plays, try running "27F." The speed with which it strikes forces the enemy to throw caution to the winds before they have fully diagnosed the play. If your blocks are carried out perfectly, the ball carrier may well be in the end zone before the opponent has figured it out completely. (See photos of this play following page 132.)

We suggest that you run this play as "46F" just as often as you use it from the opposite side. The reason for this is that on a sequence of such simple plays as this it is a good idea to keep your quarterback spinning in opposite directions as often as possible in order completely to confuse the men across the line. Should the defensive center be playing to the left of our center, it would be prudent for the faking fullback to run to the right side of the quarterback, as illustrated in the photographs. This will cause less confusion near the point of exchange.

9

The Forward Pass

WE HAVE TWO general pass plans in use at Notre Dame. The first is what we call our "11 pass series," whereas the second plan is a forward pass set-up which runs from every play that we have in our attack. The "11 pass series" means that the quarterback does the passing. In the other group, the quarterback will pass, as a rule, but he may hand off to any one of the other backs who can throw a forward pass. In our opinion, the greatest feature of the "T" formation is that there are so many passing possibilities from each running play. The opponents never know whether the man who is coming at them is a decoy, a blocker, or a pass receiver. With this element of surprise on his side, the intended receiver should be able to "shake" the man who is guarding him.

As mentioned, the quarterback does the majority of the passing in our formation. Therefore, we will limit all of our discussion of pass plays to those in which the quarterback does the throwing. When we discuss individual play we will give some hints for the use of other backfield men who may be called upon to do the passing.

PASSING TECHNIQUE

In order to become an excellent passer, the quarterback must master certain fundamentals. They must become just as much a part of him as are his walking and talking methods. After he has learned to do something correctly, he should always do it in the same way. In this manner, it will always take him about the same amount of time to perform an activity, and thus he will automatically have a perfect sense of how much time he needs to complete a play. Have your quarterback spend a great deal of time with the center with whom he will be playing in the game. As a general rule, when we substitute in a game, we like to send in a quarterback and a center at the same time, as each man does things a little bit differently from the next, and Saturday afternoon is no time for the quarterback to become accustomed to a center's way of doing business. The signal caller must make absolutely certain that he receives the ball from the center with the laces under his fingers. He should work as often as possible on just taking the ball from the center and throwing without moving. Try each pass a few times before starting a practice session.

The quarterback's eyes should never leave the field of play when he is planning to throw a pass. Naturally, if he is running back, he cannot be scrutinizing the field, but once he gets ready to pass he should have the entire playing area in his vision. He should keep a special watch on the defensive men. He knows approximately where his receivers will go, and he should look to see if that section of the field is going to be especially congested.

GRIPPING THE BALL

When he raises the ball to pass, the quarterback should hold it with both hands as long as possible. He should hold it high over his right shoulder (throughout this discussion we are assuming that the passer is right-handed), and when he throws he must throw high with a straight goalward motion. He should throw the ball as if it were a dart, turning his wrist inward so that the ball will go in a perfectly straight line. We have our passers start their passing drills down on one knee, gripping the ball on the ground and making certain the fingers cover the lacing. From here they pick the ball up, raise it over the shoulder, and throw it. Have two passers play catch from this stance until they are able to obtain a maximum amount of accuracy. Each should make a target of his hands and let the other aim at that spot. At first they will not like to throw from such a high angle, but make them do this—it is the way all the really great passers throw the ball.

DELIVERY

Prior to throwing the ball, the quarterback's feet should be rather close together—close enough so that he is comfortable while standing as tall as possible. As he begins to raise the ball to pass, he should gradually shift his weight over to his right foot. His left foot should be pointed directly at the intended receiver. The ball should not be released until the fingers of the passer are as close to the receiver as they will be. By using this straight up-and-down method, your passer will find that it is much easier to throw a perfect spiral. Many of the game's most successful passers like to fake at least one throw before they release the ball. The best method for a passer to employ when he decides to do this is to bring the ball down hard into the palm of the left hand. This will complete the maneuver and he will have the ball back in both hands ready to start all over again. An experienced passer may make one of these good hard fakes in one direction and then pivot and pass out to the other side of the field. When mastered, this trick will prove tremendously effective, but we will not delve any deeper into it, since we plan to confine ourselves to the fundamental phases.

Sidearm passes are not good because they cannot be accurate, nor can the passer throw them hard enough to avoid interception by an alert defensive team. At Notre Dame we have all of our passers spend a little time standing close to an iron bar that is suspended a few inches above the man's head and one yard in front of the passer. By making them throw continually over this bar, we find that they soon become accustomed to releasing the ball in the manner we believe best.

ACCURACY

Accuracy is the sign of a great passer. Always have your passer pick out a spot on the receiver's body as a target. Make it either his nose or ear, or if it is a stop pass (as diagrammed on page 111), throw the pigskin at the receiver's belt buckle. Keep the passer working on these targets at all times, because frequently in a tough game he will find that if he does not hit right on the target, it will be impossible for the man to get his hands on the ball.

PASS RECEIVING

Pass catching is an art that can be developed in a ballplayer but one that seems to be much more natural to some than to others. Train your boys to "look" the ball all the way into their hands. Just as in golf the player must keep his eye on the ball until he has hit it, the pass receiver is tempting lady luck if he does not keep both of his eyes on the ball every second until it is tucked away under his arm. We use the same drill for pass receivers as we do for men on the receiving end of a lateral; that is, we number all of the balls, and as soon as the man catches one we stop him and ask him what the number is. Once they have developed this habit, we ask each pass receiver to sprint at top speed for at least fifteen yards every time he catches a pass. Make this mandatory, for it gets the boys in the habit of turning on the steam as soon as they have that ball tucked away safely.

PASS PATTERNS

We have many pass patterns, the majority of which are adaptable to either the "11 pass series" or passing from our regular "T" plays. First, we shall describe all of the pass assignments that we give to our ends. Every play that can be worked with one end has its opposite with the other flanker man. When assigning these pass plays, we give each one a different name. This eliminates having to say whether the pass will be to the left end or right end every time we call such a play. For instance, when we ask our right end to run straight out for five yards and then cut in parallel to the line of scrimmage, we call that pass "11 pass parallel." When the identical play is called with the left end as the receiver, our quarterback calls for "11 pass across." This reduces the possibility of confusion in the huddle and makes it a little easier on our potential pass receivers. A question that is always raised at this time is, "Do you throw all of your passes by assignment or do you allow the quarterback to look over the field?" The answer is that we do both. As a rule, short passes are called to the specific man, but we always have an extra man available to whom the back can throw in case the intended receiver is bottled up completely.

PASSES TO THE ENDS

On page 107 are all of the assignments that we give to the ends on our squad. It does not make any difference to these linemen whether the play is run in the "11 pass series" or after one of our basic "T" plays has been faked. The call for the ends is always the same. Some of the titles may seem peculiar, but we try to give each pass a name that will bring the assignment into the mind of the player as soon as he hears it. Request each end to learn every one of these assignments for both positions, as well as the assignments we give to our backfield men. This will help to make him a better decoy.

The Angle Pass.—The first pass pattern we give to our ends is the angle pass. It is entitled "angle left" and "angle right." In the huddle our quarterback will say, "Signals, 11 pass angle right." Or if we are planning to run this pass from one of our "T" plays, he might call, "43 pass angle right." As soon as the ball is snapped, the end to whom the ball is to be thrown steps off with his outside foot at an angle of forty-five degrees to the scrimmage line and runs hard for five yards. At this point he pivots, turning away from the line

Pass patterns for both ends:

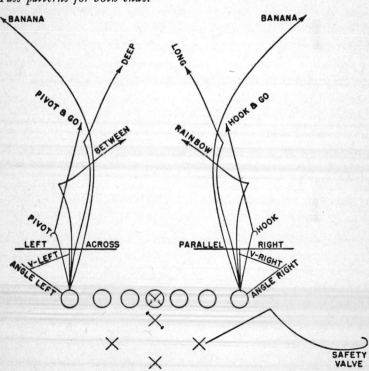

of scrimmage, and the ball should be on its way. This play is good for a small yardage situation. We often vary it by having our left end lateral out to one of the halfbacks who is coming around wide outside of the end.

The V Pass.—The second pattern, which is nothing more than an extension of the angle pass, is what we call the "V pass, left" or "right." The end takes his five steps in one direction, makes a V turn, and steps off five more toward the center of the field. This time he takes the ball over his inside shoulder. Use this against a defense that has the linebackers floating as soon as your ends make a move in any one direction.

The Parallel Pass.—Next we have the parallel pass, which we call "across" when we plan to throw to the left end. On this play the intended receiver sprints out straight for approximately seven yards before cutting on a ninety-degree angle toward the center of the field. This is a spot pass that our quarterback will throw directly over the center to a spot about seven yards past the line of scrimmage. This is a very good play, which usually should bring excellent results against a normal six-man line. Ask your ends to run as hard as they can while they go out straight. This will throw the linebackers off guard because it will appear that the ends are heading all the way down the field.

Pass Left or Right.—When "11 pass right" or "left" is called, we ask our ends to spring out the same distance as on the last play, but when they make their ninety-degree cut it should be out, toward the sidelines, rather than in. This play is also adaptable to a lateral out to the halfback should the occasion permit.

Hook and Pivot Passes.—It is "hook" for the right end or "pivot" for the left end on the next play. When this assignment is called, we have the ends dash out about eight yards past the line and then turn completely about so that they are facing the passer. The intended receiver should make the turn outward, toward the sideline, and be prepared to receive the ball somewhere in around his midsection. It is possible for the end to make a good fake on this play, thus throwing the defensive back completely off guard. If he runs up very hard, stops dead, and then pivots, he should have plenty of time to catch the pass before the halfback has stopped retreating and can get up to the spot. From this play we run what we call "hook and go," or "pivot and go." On these plays we ask the ends to complete the original assignment and then turn on the speed until they have gotten past the defending halfback. You will find that the first few times you run this in a game your ends will have an excellent chance of getting out into the clear. (See photos of "37 pass hook" following page 132.)

Long Passes.—The pass play in which we strive to have our ends get behind the safety man is called "deep" for the left end and "long" for the right end. We do not have any set method that they must follow to get down the field, but we do like to see them employ a good fake or a change of pace as they elude some of the defenders. It seems that the best pass receivers like to start out as if they were going in toward the center of the field and then begin to ease away from the safety man. On these passes we have our passer give the receiver a substantial lead, for the latter will be running at full speed and should be able to take it over his shoulder for best results.

The Banana Pass.—Whenever we call a "banana" pass, it is not called to either one of the ends specifically. The reason for calling such a play is to force the defense to spread wide open. Thus, when we call this play we want both ends to veer off in a manner that resembles the shape of a banana. As a rule, it will be very seldom that both of these men will be covered completely. If such is the case, the next time you run the same play send a receiver down the middle; he should be free since the opponent has only eleven men on the field.

The Rainbow or Between Pass.—The "rainbow" pass is to

the right end and its counterpart, the "between" pass, is to the left end.   This pass should be right down the alley.   The end should run straight out for nearly ten yards and then round in toward the center of the field on an angle that brings a rainbow to mind.   This play will work a little better if you have the opposite end running a "banana" while the man-in-motion is breaking toward the opposite sidelines.

You will notice that on all of the pass patterns we have the right halfback designated as the safety valve.   His job is to be ready to tackle anyone who may have intercepted one of our passes.   In effect, he is our safety man on pass offense.   Have him out there always, and if all of the potential receivers are covered, you can always throw the pass out to him.   Sometimes we have been mighty pleased at the results of such a forced pass play.

PASSES TO THE BACKS

Next we teach the plays used when throwing the ball to the man-in-motion.   These are diagrammed on page 111.   Any one of the three backs may be in the position of the motion man.   All that is necessary is for the signal caller to call, for example, "11 pass (Name) 2-5."   This would mean the pass play as designated, with the number two back in motion and the ball being snapped on five.

The Stop Pass.—The first assignment we will give is our "stop" pass.   If the quarterback wished to throw this pass to the fullback, he would call "11 pass stop 3-5."   On the stop pass we ask the man-in-motion to cut toward the goal line as soon as the ball is snapped.   He should sprint up to a spot about seven yards past the line of scrimmage and then pivot out toward the sideline, coming completely around so that his belt buckle is facing the passer.   This play can also be run as a "stop and go," in which case the intended receiver, after completing the above movements, would turn back and run downfield until he had gotten behind the defensive halfback.

The Flare Passes.—We have both a "flare-in" and a "flare-out," which are fairly well described by their titles. When the back is about seven yards past the line of scrimmage he breaks at an angle of about forty-five degrees, in or out, whatever the case may be. When acting as a decoy on passes to the end, it is usually a good thing for the man-in-motion to execute a flare-out maneuver. When he does this, he not only draws a defender out with him, but he also makes certain that he will not run into the man for whom the pass is intended.

The Up Pass.—The "up" pass is between a "flare-in" and a "stop" pass. The man proceeds about ten yards down the

Pass patterns to the man-in-motion:

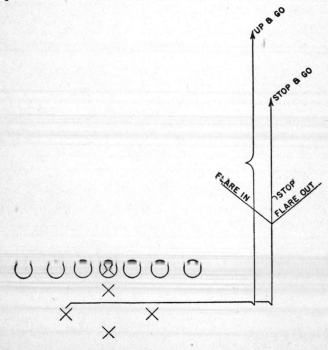

field and cuts in for about two steps.   This is a quick-working pass, which we have found to be quite effective despite its simplicity.   From the "up" pass we also run an "up and go," which works on the same principle as the "stop and go" pass.

HELPFUL HINTS FOR THE PASSING ATTACK

We have found that when facing a six- or seven-man line the best bet is to use the "11 pass series" because these plays strike more quickly and there are not too many men in the defensive backfield to interfere.   However, when we hit a five-man line, it is a different story.   As soon as the enemy see the quarterback fading to pass, it seems that every zone on the field is covered.   This is when we run our pass pattern from the everyday "T" plays.   It is difficult to say which play works best into our passing system, but I believe the one we like to use the most is our "29H pass."   It seems that by the time the backers-up see the quarterback starting to throw his lateral out to the left halfback, they are convinced that it is going to be a running play.   It is then that we have the quarterback fake that lateral and fade back to pass to any one of our eligible receivers.

We require all of our potential pass receivers at Notre Dame to know what each and every eligible pass receiver does on every pass play.   We demand this because we do not feel that a man can act as a successful decoy if he does not know what the actual receiver is supposed to do on the play.   Teach your decoy men to study the pass defense system being used by the opponents.   If they look this over carefully, they should be able to devise a plan whereby the enemy pass protectors will be drawn out of the zone where the quarterback intends to throw the pass.   Just like everything else in football, it takes lots of teamwork to make a forward pass play successful.

A very helpful maneuver on pass plays is to spread your end wide on the side opposite that toward which the man-in-motion will run.   The enemy will then have to widen its defense to such an extent that it should be extremely vulnerable down the middle. Always try throwing one or two passes to these men who are spread, in order to let your opponent know that they are not out there just for decoy purposes.

We have found that to try a forward pass on the first play of the game is one of the most disconcerting things that can face the opponent. In our game with Iowa in 1946 we initiated the play with a touchdown pass from John Lujack to Terry Brennan. It was a long pass to the left halfback, who had gone in motion and was behind the Iowa secondary before they realized it. Ever since that contest we have felt that it was this surprise movement that allowed our team to hand Iowa its worst defeat of that season. They were an excellent team, but our lads were fortunate enough to get the jump on them and were never headed after that opening play.

Do not use your passes if you do not have to. When your running game is going well, save your pass plays for later in the year. Many times our passes will click perfectly against one team, and the following Saturday they just do not seem to be working out. It is at this time that you should have a good, solid running game to fall back on. Each style of play is of utmost importance in football, and if you have them both, you will have a good team. We think that one of the main reasons Johnny Lujack had so much success as a passer was because he was such a terrific running threat. The defense could not just allow him to stand back and throw, because if they did, he would run with the ball as he did against Purdue in 1947, when he carried twenty-seven yards for a touchdown after finding all the receivers covered.

An important *must* for all potential pass receivers is that they do not tip off the play in their eagerness to rush out and catch the ball. This is especially important with the ends. Many times they will find that an opponent is in a very good spot to "jam" our end as he starts out to receive a pass. If such is the case, we ask our boys to get the jump on the enemy.

As soon as the ball is snapped the end should charge across the line and force his shoulder into the opponent. This need only take a second, because when he sees the end means business his main concern will be to throw off the block and get into our backfield. This not only opens up the road for the receiver to go downfield, but it also throws the opponent off guard. If players will keep in mind that all good performances are done step by step, they will have little trouble in completing any type of play.

Receivers are told that they should run at four-fifths of their top speed when they are going out for a pass. This will enable them to turn on an additional amount after they have the pigskin in their possession. This reserve will help to disconcert the defensive backfield and will make it possible for the receiver to go all the way. Train your boys not to attempt to catch the ball until it is ready to be caught. Instruct them to "look" it all the way into their hands. They should not stretch out to get it. It will come in by itself. When caught, the hands should be on the far end of the ball. Relaxation is one of the most important phases of pass catching. If the receiver can just keep his mind on the idea of catching the ball as if he were in pass practice, he will have little difficulty. He should never worry about the tacklers until he has the ball tucked under his arm. They will give him very little trouble if he does not have the ball, so they should not cause him to be nervous.

Pass catchers should always keep their hands as high as possible when running downfield. This will give the passer something at which to shoot. On long passes the entire body of the potential receiver should be facing the goal line, with only his head turned so that he is looking directly at the passer. This is a trick which takes some training, but one that must be learned to become a good pass receiver. When a man can master this method of running, he can usually elude the safety man long enough to receive the ball fom his quarterback.

If we run into bad weather during the practice sessions, we have our men move into the fieldhouse. We ask all of our pass receivers to put on basketball shoes and gather on the basketball court. We place the lads under one of the baskets and have our passers throw the ball at the backboard. Just as a basketball coach has his men work to get the rebounds, we have our receivers go in the air to get the ball as it bounces crazily off the board. This is excellent practice, for it breaks the boys of a very bad habit. Many receivers are excellent until the ball is hit by the opponent, and then they forget about it. However, if your boys have had this training on the backboards, they will automatically react in a very different manner. We tell the men that we do not want to see the ball hit the floor. There is a great deal of scrambling after the pigskin, but we find it pays enormous dividends on Saturday afternoon. In our Northwestern game of 1947 Frank Tripucka had thrown a very long pass to our reserve halfback, Lancaster Smith. At least three men got between Smitty and the ball, and it looked as if it were impossible for him even to see where it was going, let alone catch it. The speedster from Lebanon, Kentucky, never took his eyes off the ball, and before the Northwestern secondary knew exactly where it had landed, our halfback had carried it over the goal line.

EIGHT ESSENTIALS

We have laid down eight rules that we feel are absolutely fundamental in order to have a successful pass offense. Some are obvious, some are repetitious, but *all eight are necessary* if you intend to make good use of your passing game.

First, every man on the squad must have that burning

desire to see the pass completed. If so much as one man lets up in this respect, the pass may be blocked, intercepted, or the passer thrown for a loss.

Second, we must have blocking. Protection will be covered in the next chapter, so we will not go into it at this time.

The third is obvious. You must have a good passer. If you do not have one, make one. The majority of backs have a general idea of how to pass, and if the coaches are willing to pay the price of working daily with a few young men, they will find that success always comes to those who are willing to sacrifice enough of their time to make something of someone else. There is no better feeling than that which comes from being able to sit on the bench on a Saturday afternoon and feel, deep down in your heart, that your efforts played some little part in the outstanding performance that certain lads are putting on out in front of you.

Fourth, you must have capable pass receivers. Not one, but as many as you can find. The more good receivers you have, the harder it will be for an opponent to cover them.

Fifth, you must have a good running game to support your passing attack. Good passing can carry a team all the way down the field, but when they get close to the goal, they will stall if their running attack will not function. When you get close to the goal, the space in which to complete passes is extremely limited. Neglect of the running fundamentals has caused the downfall of some of the greatest teams in the nation.

Sixth is up to the quarterback. The more stress he puts on deception, the better chance the play will have of clicking. Have him work just as hard to make it look like a run as he possibly can. In passing, as in any phase of the game, it is much easier to fake a man out than to block him out of the play.

Seventh, everyone who is close to the ball should block for the receiver. Have your blockers keep their eyes open; as

soon as they see anyone who might slow down production they should "fly" between the receiver and the potential tackler.

Eighth is cleverness. This applies to all eleven men who are on the field. If each man does his best to work quickly and cleverly with the team's interest at heart, he will find that the pass plays are working exceptionally well. Some linemen tend to loaf on a pass play because they feel it is out of their jurisdiction. Let me assure you that if we ever detect such a habit in any of our players, we never detect it a second time in the same man. We feel at Notre Dame that we do not have time to waste on men who are not desirous of putting out 100 percent for sixty minutes on Saturday and for the required practice time during the week. It is very seldom that we run into this attitude on our squad, since we try extremely hard to drive away such men by means of our "Get Acquainted Talk," before we issue any uniforms.

As a last word on passing, we wish to remind you to have your passer keep the ball high. His arm should complete a perfect arc and his left toe points in the direction toward which he is passing. Have him practice these maneuvers by playing catch as often as possible with another passer. Good passers can be made!

10

Protecting the Passer

A PRIME REQUISITE for successful passing is that the passer have confidence in his teammates. He must feel certain that he is going to have plenty of time to get the ball away and that the potential tacklers will not get to him soon enough to ruin his accuracy. To develop this assuredness requires a great deal of time and hard work during the practice periods. Each man has a positive assignment on our pass protection set-up. We will illustrate the pass protection pattern that we have found to be most successful. Believe me when I say that we have tried innumerable variations to allow the passer as much time as possible, and we feel that the one we are going to describe has brought the best results.

In view of the fact that our backs have been exceptionally small, the only one we ask to do the blocking is the fullback. This is the principal reason why we look for a fullback who is rather heavy. When the pass is going to be thrown to the fullback, it becomes necessary for us to do one of two things. The first, and the one we employ most often, is to sacrifice one of our ends as a pass receiver or decoy, and have him block the opposing end. An alternative is to have your right halfback take care of the end. Most backs have the necessary desire to perform this task, but it is extremely difficult for a 165 pound back to block a 210-pound end long enough for the passer to throw the ball. At times when passes are absolutely necessary it is wise to have two of your larger backs in the game for the purpose of protecting the passer.

ASSIGNMENTS FOR PROTECTING THE PASSER

BASIC PLAN: AGAINST A SIX-MAN LINE

The pattern that is outlined on page 120 is our basic pass protection set-up. Working from this plan, we make any minor changes that become necessary in order to fit a given situation.

We ask our men to carry out, as nearly as possible, the following instructions when the ball is snapped. The *right end* should sprint directly downfield to assume whatever receiver's position is required for the particular play. In the diagram, where the men are opposing a normal six-man line, it is possible for the end to run right out without having to cope with any enemy linemen.

The *right tackle* should try to make one fast step across the line and then start to come up high for his block. A pass block should always be high because it screens the passer and allows the blocker to keep working on the enemy until the ball is thrown. The offensive man should always block his opponent out from the center. If the defensive man gets to the inside, he has too great an opportunity to fake the blocker and knife in toward the passer. A cardinal rule for pass blockers is never to allow the defensive man to get behind them or inside of them, either by charging or by means of a fake. The lineman has time and, if necessary, it is all right for him to give ground to the enemy. The passer is a considerable distance behind the line and, so long as the enemy does not penetrate all the way back there, he is safe. Your blocker should start working high on the man and just keep scuffling with him until the ball has been released by the passer. If necessary, have your tackle go all the way to the ground with the enemy and keep driving from his hands and knees.

The *right guard's* assignment is similar to that of the tackle on the same side.   Provided he gets the initial jump on the man across the line, he should be able to keep bumping him until the play has gone down in history.

The *center*, who has a man to his left, should be certain to get across the line as soon as the ball is snapped.   The angle on this block is not too good because of the space between the

Protecting the passer.   "11 Pass series" against a six-man line.   The passer has a choice of spinning either to the right or to the left prior to retreating:

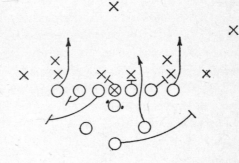

Protecting the passer.   "43 Pass series" against a six-man line:

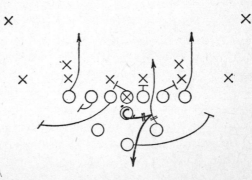

men. Therefore it is required that the center operate just as fast as he possibly can. Let him work hard with the man, driving him out toward the sideline. He, too, should employ every possible method to insure that the man does not cross into the backfield.

The *left guard* of the offensive team has a somewhat different assignment to perform. We have him pull back so as to be in a waiting spot for the defensive right end as he comes across the line. Have the guard pull rapidly so that he can assume an advantageous blocking angle before the end gathers too much speed. It may be necessary to block this end back toward our own goal line, but so long as he is removed from the danger zone, that is all we ask.

The *left tackle* also pulls on this play, but his man is much closer and thus he must work even faster than the guard. Make certain that it is impossible for the opposing tackle to come inside of your tackle. When the "down" is called the left tackle should edge in toward the guard on his side. This will leave a large hole that will look inviting to the defending tackle. Most likely he will try to charge through as soon as the ball is snapped. If he does use this method, it is very easy for our left tackle to be in a good blocking position when the enemy comes across the line.

The *left end's* assignment will vary according to the pass pattern that is called.

Now for the backfield play. We have our *quarterback* place his feet as indicated by the dots on the chart. This is an assignment that will vary with the direction of the pass. On the "11 pass" group we have the quarterback turn to his right each time. That is, he makes a partial pivot and then runs back to his passing pocket. If the pass is called from the "43" plan, we have the quarterback place his feet in the same manner as on that play. On an "11 pass" we allow our passer to change the position of his feet occasionally if he is throwing many passes in any one game. This keeps the opponents guessing and does not place any undue hardship on the signal caller.

The diagram we have drawn on page 120 is for a pass to the right side of the field. Whenever we are passing in that direction, we have our *fullback* take the end on that side. If the pass is to the left, we have the number three back block the opposing end in that area. This makes it possible for our onside end to move down into a position where he can catch the ball. In order to prevent this move from "tipping off" the enemy, we have our fullback take the opposite end at any time when we have called for a definite pass plan. That is, if we plan to pass to the right halfback, we have the right end take the enemy wingman while the fullback is working on the other side of the line.

To illustrate the above system we have diagrammed our "22 pass" as well as our "11 pass left" on page 123. These simple passes, like the basic running plays, will mean more to a successful "T" than all of the trick pass plays that have ever been called. Simplicity wins football games.

PROTECTING FOR "11 PASS LEFT" AGAINST THE 5-3-2-1

When a pass is called against a 5-3-2-1 set-up, we are able to send both of our *ends* into the enemy secondary. Of course the opponents have more men back there, but good pass catchers should be able to operate successfully against such a plan. In the diagram, we simply have them running down for ten yards and stopping; however, this plan may be changed for any pass we desire to throw.

The *right tackle* should take one fast step in the direction of the man to his right, and then come up fast with a high shoulder block. After the initial contact is made he should be willing to give a little ground before he blocks the man again. If he will continue to bump this man for five or six times, the passer should have ample time to get rid of the ball.   These tall blocks should be very aggressive and should actually make the enemy retreat a little bit each time except the first.

Our *right guard* must pull quickly and prevent the enemy end from entering our backfield.   Drill your guards on pulling exceptionally rapidly, because if they can get the jump on the end, they should have no trouble in keeping him out of the play.

The *center* has a man on his head, and he should scuffle with

Protecting the passer.   "11 Pass left" against the 5-3-2-1:

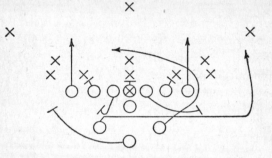

"22 Pass series" against the 5-3-2-1:

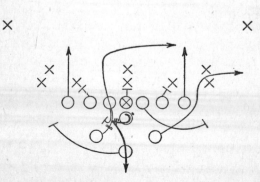

him until certain the ball is in the air. We ask the center as soon as the ball leaves his hands to drive his shoulder into the man across the line. He should then take one step back and come up tall. This will put him in a position to stop the second onslaught of his opponent. There is no excuse for a man ever getting past the center to block a pass.

There is no definite opponent for our *left guard* to deal with, so we ask him to come up fast and retreat gradually, looking in all directions for a potential tackler. This man should come back like a cat, with his eyes covering the entire enemy line. The instant he sees a man break away from one of our blockers, he should brace himself to stop that man from advancing any further.

The *left tackle* must get the jump on the man to his left in order to keep this enemy from breaking through. The angle is fairly sharp, and it will take some fast maneuvering to bump him out of the play.

We have discovered that it is always helpful to send a man-in-motion on a pass play. This little gesture causes the enemy to spread their defense, which makes them that much more vulnerable to a pass down the middle. Whether it be an "11 pass" or a pass from one of your regular "T" plays, you will be very wise to send a man-in-motion. Frequently when we run the "22 pass" we have the right halfback go in motion rather than fake a "48H." When this is done, it gives greater importance to the fake between the quarterback and the left halfback. If these two men will strive diligently to deceive the enemy, we might find ourselves to be a passing power.

PASS BLOCKS: TEN ESSENTIALS

Blocking, like every other phase of football, depends mainly on how well your men learn the fundamentals. We have set down ten requirements that we feel must be adhered to by every member of a team that expects to get anywhere in the air.

First, and foremost, is that every man must possess that *burning desire* to block the opponent. Without this willingness to scuffle with the man across the line, no man will ever be of any great assistance to his teammate who is trying to locate a receiver downfield.

Second, we do not want our men to become aggressive too soon. The lineman who is too aggressive is likely to go past his man and thus leave the path clear all the way to the passer. We like our men to make the first move and then retreat a little. Not until they are certain that they have the man on the ropes should they really start to dig in and drive him away from the action area.

Third, we do not want any tip-offs. Too many linemen prefer not to get all the way down if they are going to use a pass block. We insist that every man go through the exact same motions on every play until the actual second when he must make his vital move.

Fourth, we like to have the enemy show his hand first. It is easy to discover whether the enemy plans to crash or wait. As soon as our man sees this he works accordingly; that is, he should stop a crashing man with a hard shoulder block and then come up tall, ready to scuffle with him. A waiting tackle will be slow coming across, and it might be well to jump at him and then spring back into a retreating stance.

The fifth requirement will help to make pass protection much easier; that is, to take the charge out of your opponent. As soon as he starts, hit him. Once he has lost his initial charge it will take him a few seconds to start a second drive, and by this time the ball should be on its way down the field.

Sixth, we want our men to recover immediately. Should they make a mistake on any of the foregoing points, they must get right back in the fight and put their whole body into an effort to protect the passer.

Seventh, they should keep fighting their men until there is absolutely no chance of their doing any harm to the passer. No matter how long the passer takes, his teammates should stick with their men.

Eighth, a change of tactics makes things a lot easier. If the enemy does not know how you plan to block him, he will not know how to combat your tactics. Variety is difficult to cope with.

Ninth, all blockers should try to "ride" their opponents out and back from the passer. They should form a pocket and not let anyone inside of it.

Tenth, and last, each and every pass blocker should be extremely relaxed. This is one play where the enemy must come to you—just wait for him and then block him.

11

Quarterback Play

REQUISITES FOR QUARTERBACKS

WHEN WE LOOK OVER our group of quarterback candidates, the first thing we search for in the young men is character. We like to have a lad running our team who is the type that is looked up to wherever he is seen. We feel that it is a great honor to be the quarterback on a football team, and we want to be certain that the young man is deserving of such acclaim. In this man must be that inherent *desire* to win ball games. His spirit permeates the entire squad. If he thinks only in terms of winning, then you will find that such a thought will be in the mind of every member of your team. We require this in every man, but it must be an outstanding characteristic in the signal caller.

The man we place over our center must have a tremendous amount of analytical ability. He must be able to surmise at one quick glance what type of defense the enemy is going to use, and in the same instant he must decide what play will work best against what the opponent sets up.

Self-confidence must be exceptionally prevalent in your quarterback—not to the extent of cockiness, but enough so that all the members of the team will hold him high in their esteem and be ready to hop the moment he calls the signal.

Intelligence goes hand in hand with confidence, because he must know what to do before he can know that he is doing the right thing. Have him study the team thoroughly and know each and every player. If he knows the capabilities of all the lads, he will know also how much he can get out of each one when things are going rough in a big game.

Leadership and poise must be notable qualities in this lad, since it is his task to lead a group of educated, talented young men through nine or ten very busy Saturday afternoons. He must develop the ability to give orders with a firm manner that will instill the necessary confidence in his teammates. He must have a reason for running every play, and when this reason is convincing to him he should carry out his thoughts without the slightest hesitation. When he is outside the huddle he should make up his mind definitely as to what play he is going to call, and once he steps inside he should be the complete master of the situation. He should call the play just as if he were a military man giving a brisk command. Have him speak out so that every member of the team can hear him plainly. Pronunciation is a very important part of signal calling because the names of so many plays sound alike unless specifically called.

When considering a man for this position, you should try to select one who is an excellent ball handler, a good faker, and who has passing ability. True, you can work for hours and develop these qualities in a man if necessary, but as a rule, you will find that a few members of your squad do possess such attributes; the best way is to capitalize on the natural ability that is inherent in these men.

When your quarterback is not in the practice scrimmage, have him stand by and study his teammates. By doing this, he may notice, for example, that the right tackle has exceptional ability when blocking to his right but is a little weak when operating to his left. Some time in a game when things are mighty tough it might pay touchdown dividends to have such information at his finger tips. At every opportunity have him think in terms of what he would do under various game conditions. Who is the best pass catcher? Who is the fastest starting back? Who runs the hardest? All of these little things will help the quarterback immeasurably if he has them in a mental notebook before the first game of the season. A coach can teach for hour after hour, but once the eleven men go on the field, their success lies completely in the hands of the man calling the plays.

Prior to any game the quarterback should inquire from the scouts as to the defensive merits of the opponents. Every bit of information he obtains should be carefully digested and catalogued for future reference. Any little tips that the quarterback can get before entering a contest should be thought over thoroughly and tested fairly early in the game. As soon as the game begins he should start to analyze the defensive set-up of the enemy. Have him try a few basic plays and see how they react to them. He should watch the defense as these plays unfold and keep any information he gains fresh in his mind.

A quarterback must know when to pass. We give the signal caller the following tips on when we think a pass will click:

a. Occasionally on a first down.

b. When there is a big yardage situation.

c. Any time when he notices a glaring defect in the pass defense.

d. When there is a concentration of power in the line.

e. When our running attack is stalled.

f. If it looks as if the opponent is tiring.

g. Against a sophomore pass defender.

h. If the wind is behind us.

i. With thirty or forty seconds remaining and we are in striking distance of the goal line.

When it is second down and one yard to go, we like to have

our quarterback try some of our long-gainer plays. Plays such as "29H" or "39 lateral" would be good ones to run at this time. It might also be advisable to run a sacrifice play just to obtain information as to how the enemy will react to certain maneuvers by the offensive aggregation.

Many press men refer to the quarterback as the "T Master," and that is a well-deserved title. In our system the quarterback must be the positive master of the "T." We require that he know the system from A to Z. We want him to know every assignment of every man on our team. He has to know when to punt and when not to punt; whether to punt long and straight or whether to angle for the sideline. All of these things must become an integral part of the quarterback's thoughts.

We like a quarterback who is daring, one who has imagination and likes to use it. He has to please the crowd as well as the coach. By that we do not mean that we want a "grandstander," but we do desire a man who has initiative and willingness to make an outstanding move.

A mixed offense is a hard one with which to cope. Too many signal callers will continue to run the same plays if they are working satisfactorily. This is a mistake, because they may be your "bread and butter" plays, and by the time you get down to the goal line where you will really need them, the defense will have figured out a way to stop them. It is not necessary to run many different plays, but run as many variations as possible. When an individual back is "hot," use him as much as possible—not always from the same play, but changing them around, tending to use most the ones with which he seems to have the best results. For some unexplainable reason it seems that every back looks better running from some one play than he does from all others. The quarterback must be one of the first to notice this and capitalize on it. When a back has been tackled exceptionally hard, allow him to have a little rest. There are three running backs; no one should ever be overworked.

Common sense should guide the signal caller. A stubborn man is of no help to the offense. The quarterback should listen to his teammates who have gone out as decoys and be receptive to their suggestions. We do not want them to run the team, but special attention should be given to what they have to say.

When a new back comes into the game, do not feed the ball to him for a few plays. He will be "tagged" on the *first few plays*, and until he gets the battle fever we would rather he be used as a decoy or a blocker.

During the time out periods the quarterback should think continually about his own offense so that he can force the opponents into using the defense he wants to face. This can be accomplished by figuring out just how the enemy reacts to the movements of his teammates. When he has this all clear in his mind, he is in a most enviable position. Sometimes this may take three periods to accomplish, but once it happens, your offense should start to roll.

The quarterback should be fully cognizant of his position on the field at all times. He should know how far he is from each sideline and how much time he has left in the period.

We ask the quarterback to think just as hard when playing defense as he does when he has the ball. He should ask himself what he would call under the identical circumstances. When it appears that the opponents are running what he expects, he should start to move in and curtail their activities. A quarterback can help immeasurably on defense because he sees things from exactly the right viewpoint for solving the problem.

MECHANICAL PLAY OF THE QUARTERBACK

I should like to suggest to all coaches that when they start their quarterbacks drilling on the "T" formation fundamentals, they should do so on a basketball court rather than on the turf. I know for certain that we are correct about this; we have tried every method in the book, and we find that the new quarterbacks learn just about five times as quickly inside as they do on the football field. There are several reasons for this. Our boys get far greater traction when wearing sneakers, and thus they develop much more confidence in themselves when performing their spins and cuts. It is necessary to receive a little encouragement in the early stages, and this can be accomplished much easier on the hard floor. The second point about learning indoors is, we have noticed beyond a shadow of any doubt, that when we start working on long laterals the quarterbacks can throw them much more accurately indoors. This is due to the fact that there is little or no air resistance in the gym. We are firmly convinced that every coach who tries this indoor method will concur 100 percent with our sentiments before his season has ended.

STANCE

Now, the stance of our "T" formation quarterback. As we have said before, we have worked hard at this method for many years and we can truthfully say that from our point of view it is the best of which we know. First of all, we like to have our "T" quarterbacks stand rather tall because they can observe more easily. The man should be loose and relaxed at all times. Impress upon the lads how important it is for them to stay completely relaxed. They are the lifeline of the "T." If they tighten up, the entire offense chokes.

We want the quarterback to bend his knees slightly. There is no definite reason for this, but we have noticed that every one of our great "T" quarterbacks—Bertelli, Lujack, Ratterman, and Tripucka—does business better when his knees are pointed inward. It seems to help them to move faster on their spins.

The author and Johnny Lujack, the greatest all-around football player it has been my privilege to coach.

Quarterback Tripucka has taken the ball from the center and is about to fake a handoff to fullback Mike Swistowicz, as left halfback Coy McGee starts to come into the play. The left guard begins to pull out of the line for the purpose of trapping the enemy.

The fake to the fullback has been completed and Tripucka is getting ready to feed the ball to the left halfback. The left guard is now behind his own right guard and is eyeing the man to be trapped. The enemy linemen are temporarily "frozen," since the ball is completely concealed.

McGee forms a pocket to take the ball. The quarterback is low and his activities are screened by the linemen. The left guard is about to bury his shoulder in the enemy tackle, while the offensive right tackle, 63, cuts through the line to remove the offside linebacker, 71.

The ball carrier is through the line as the hole opens wide. Note our left guard scuffling with the enemy tackle. Our right tackle is driving the offside linebacker away from the play. McGee is looking over the field to decide which way he will cut.

Photos by Jim Ferstel

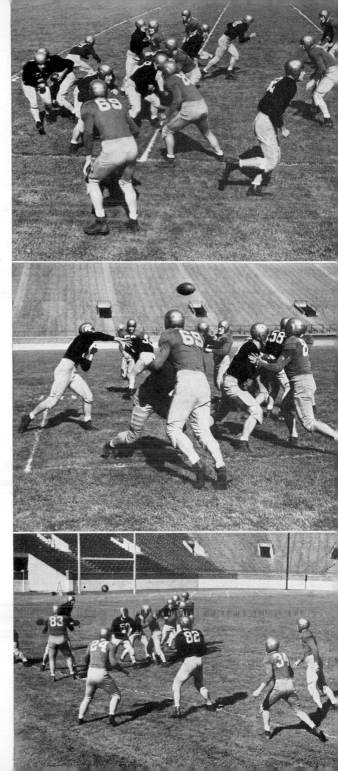

Quarterback Tripucka has made a reverse pivot to his left, and is faking to fullback Swistowicz, who is heading toward the defensive left end to fake an ordinary "37" and block on the end. Our ends, Leon Hart, 82, and Jim Martin, 38, streak downfield.

The ball is in the air and the fullback is driving hard into the enemy end. Our tackle is bringing his elbows up on the opposing tackle, who is trying to stave him off with a forearm shiver. Tripucka's arm follows the path of the pigskin.

Hart has completed his pivot and is waiting for the ball to arrive. The offensive linemen are still scuffling with the opponents. The two enemy defenders have realized too late what the play is and cannot get up in time to stop the pass.

Photos by Jim Ferstel

Photo by Jim Ferstel

1946 NATIONAL CHAMPIONS

R.E. Jack Zilly, R.T. Ziggy Czarobski, R.G. John Mastrangelo, C. George Strohmeyer, L.G. Bill Fischer, L.T. George Connor, L.E. Jim Martin. Q.B John Lujack, L.H. Terry Brennan, F.B. Jim Mello, R.H. Emil Sitko.

Defensive stance of right end Leon Hart. The right foot is back in order to allow him to push himself in when he senses the play.

Favorite defensive stance of right tackle Ziggy Czarobski. It is an excellent stance for a waiting tackle.

1947 NATIONAL CHAMPIONS

R.E. Leon Hart, R.T. Ziggy Cza-robski, R.G. Marty Wendell, C. Bill Walsh, L.G. Bill Fischer, L.T. George Connor, L.E. Jim Martin. R.H. Emil Sitko, F.B John "Pep" Panelli, Q.B. John Lujack, L.H. Terry Brennan.

The offensive stance of our 1948 Captain, left guard Bill Fischer, is similar to that of the tackle (next page), but the guard should be some-what lower.

Defensive stance used by right guard Marty Wendell when he may have to move with the play. This man backs up our line in a five-man defense, and we want him ready to move at all times.

Frank Tripucka, Notre Dame quarterback, holds the ball ready to pass. Note that his eyes are looking in the direction that his left arm is pointing.

Offensive stance of a T formation center, illustrated by Walter Grothaus. Note the position of hands and feet. Also, see how his head is up.

Offensive stance of left tackle George (Moose) Connor. The position of the feet allows him to spring into action with the ball.

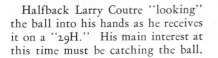

Halfback Larry Coutre "looking" the ball into his hands as he receives it on a "29H." His main interest at this time must be catching the ball.

Offensive stance of left end Jim Martin. His eyes are straight to the front and it is impossible to tell whether he plans to block the man opposite him or go down for a pass.

QUICK OPENER

Quarterback Tripucka hands to right halfback Sitko on a simple "43." Both endeavor to conceal what is happening. Left halfback McGee is just starting on his fake of "29H."

The quick opener allows Sitko to churn through the line. Please note especially quarterback Tripucka making an excellent fake to left halfback McGee in the background.

Photos by Jim Ferstel

SCORING THREAT

Frank Tripucka, quarterback, faking to the fullback, who charges into the center of the line with the pocket completely hidden to confuse the enemy.

Tripucka has brought the ball into his stomach, and is now passing it out again to left halfback McGee. Notice how the ball is just resting in the quarterback's hand. All the ball carrier has to do is "look" it into his hands and head through the line.

Photos by Jim Ferstel

THE HANDS

Now, as to the position of the hands. We want the right hand pressing hard and upward against the center's buttocks. Just enough pressure so that the center will know exactly where to put the ball is ideal. Always insist that your quarterback curl up his fingers slightly. If he does this, there will be less danger of a fumble. When the fingers are curled up, the palm is automatically forced down, which is the ideal position for the hand when the ball comes in from the center. The wrist should be turned just slightly to the right. This keeps the thumb from dropping down and spoiling the exchange. Drill the center and quarterback together just as often as you can. At the start of the practice sessions you should have the quarterback taking the ball in his right hand alone. He should not bother to use both hands until he can do it perfectly with one. This drill will instill confidence in the men, and also will guarantee that the quarterback's hand is in exactly the correct position, because if it is not, he cannot hold onto the ball with the one hand. Moreover, when the quarterback is able to take the ball in one hand, you know that the center is passing the ball back perfectly. While the men are doing this, the coach should check every time to see if the ball is coming back in such a position that the fingers of the quarterback's right hand are over the lacings when he takes it. It may be necessary for the center to turn the ball a bit, to the right or left, or it may have to be tilted either forward or backward. Make adjustments until the ball is being received just as prescribed. When the ball comes back in this manner, it is no trouble for the quarterback to spin and lateral out to one of his halfbacks.

After the boy has completely mastered this one hand movement, we start to acquaint him with what he must do with his left hand.   We want the thumbs together, but not even—that is to say, we slide the thumb of the right hand over the thumb of the left hand so that the small knuckle joint of the right thumb rests in the indentation between the two knuckle joints of the left thumb.   This sounds complicated, but if you will just place your two thumbs together, with the palm of your left hand facing the sky and the palm of the right facing the ground, and then slide the right one back until it fits flush against the left thumb, then you will have the position we desire.   Our quarterback's left hand should be turned slightly.   The reason for this is that the center automatically twists the ball every time he snaps it. This is a natural tendency that cannot be changed; we make amends by having the back turn his hand.

When the boys are practicing their automatic exchange with two hands you do not have to see it to know whether or not it is a good one.   You can hear it for quite some distance. There should be a real bang!   Pop, pop, pop, should be the only sound you hear when your ball handlers are warming up before practice.   If you cannot hear it, something is wrong.   You may be saying, "Well why?   What is the importance of getting the ball back so hard?"   Our answer to this is that nothing can be accomplished until the quarterback has the ball.   He cannot spin, fake, pass, or even move until he gets the ball.   Now, if the center will drive the ball back just as hard and as fast as he possibly can, the quarterback will be able to commence his operations that much sooner. This will mean that our ball carriers can reach their holes sooner; they can line up closer to the line of scrimmage because it will not take so long for the ball to get to them.   It is hard to visualize, but this speedy little maneuver by the center can make the difference between an average team and a truly great team.   We have a silly offer that we make at the outset of our spring and fall drills every year.   We tell all of our centers that we will buy a new suit for every center who can draw blood from the quarterback's hand when he snaps the ball back. You can tell the center 1,000 times to snap the ball back fast, but the way really to impress them is to say that you want to see blood on the quarterback's hands.

PIVOTS

The first pivot we work on is called our reverse pivot. It is the most important pivot in our system, since we use it on almost all of our basic plays. As previously mentioned, whenever we diagram a play, we always put little dots to designate the position of the quarterback's feet when the play starts. The following instructions are those that we give to our quarterback for his performance in play number "43." Most all other plays work from this basic procedure, whether they be to the right or the left. As soon as he receives the ball from the center the quarterback should bring it in to his stomach. This is item number one, and we do not want our quarterback to come away from the center until he has brought the ball all the way into his stomach. As soon as he has the ball in close we want him to spin just as fast as he can. This spin adds speed and deception to the play because everybody loses sight of the ball temporarily. You know who has it. The defensive men realize where the ball is, but because it is impossible for them to see it, we believe that a great deal more deception is added to the play. The faster the spin, the more effective it will be. Your quarterback can learn to spin faster by learning to twist with his shoulder. His shoulder starts him out, and his left foot gives him a push-off. Now follow this carefully. He pushes hard with his left foot, and he twists very hard with his shoulder. He gets the ball and spins around to a position in which he is facing the sideline that was on his right when the play started. This puts him in the proper spot to step out and hand the

ball to the right halfback. Ask your quarterback to complete his pivot with his head up and his back straight. If
the quarterback is all hunched over, he will find that the
halfback is likely to run into him when he speeds in to take
the ball. He must work at length with the halfbacks in
order that he and the potential ball carrier will meet at the
proper time. Try as you may, it will be late in the season before this perfect timing is worked out between your quarterback and the remaining members of the backfield. On the
"opposite" plays the quarterback's left foot is back and he
spins in the opposite direction.

The thing that has given our quarterbacks the greatest
amount of assistance with regard to this reverse pivot is the
position of the left foot at the completion of the turn. When
we first installed the "T" we found that our quarterbacks
always were off balance when they completed their pivot.
We had always asked them to make certain that the toes of
both feet were pointing toward the sideline. It was this that
threw them completely out of gear. By means of the trial
and error method, with which every football coach is very
familiar, we learned to tell our quarterbacks that when they
come around they should plant their left foot with the toes
at an angle of about forty-five degrees. In other words,
instead of the toes facing the sideline, they should be turned
in the direction of the opponent's goal line by about forty-
five degrees. Any boy can stop like that. We sincerely believe that this little suggestion has helped our quarterbacks
more than anything else in the mechanical line.

Next, we ask our quarterback to line up, not with his
elbows outstretched, but with them in fairly close to his side.
Neither the hands, the arms, nor the elbows should be stiff,
since it may be necessary for them to give just a bit with the
center. As the center pulls away, it may be necessary for the
quarterback to "ride" the ball with him for a fraction of an

inch, something that could not be accomplished with stiff elbows.

HANDING OFF

When the quarterback spins around he should look, not at the potential ball carrier, but at the man to whom he plans to fake. For instance, if he plans to feed to the right halfback on a "43," he should be looking at the left halfback as he spins around. Make it the definite responsibility of the halfback to come in and take the ball from the quarterback, rather than the latter going out and giving it to the halfback. He should hold the ball out with his feeding hand on the bottom. The reason for this is that if the feeding hand is so placed it is impossible for the quarterback to slam it into the ball carrier's midsection. If he holds the ball any other way, he might have a tendency to throw it in there too hard, thus making it difficult for the running back to grasp it. In our method the quarterback is not watching the runner, but is just standing there with the ball lying in his feeding hand. As the runner comes in to take the ball, the feeding hand should give for about six inches with the ball carrier. That is, the quarterback's feeding hand goes in the direction of the number three hole.

On a play such as "29H," when we ask our quarterback to make a complete fake of "43," he should make each move exactly as we have described for the quick-opener. As the halfback comes by, we want the ball to be pushed right into his stomach, and then drawn back easily. Then as the halfback hunches over to shield the pocket, the quarterback should step out in the direction of the left halfback. When the quarterback begins his pitchout to the left half, he should do so right from the stomach. Too many laterals are thrown by the quarterback drawing his arm back as if he were pitching a softball.   When this method is employed there is a possibility that someone may slip up behind him and steal the ball, or if not this, it becomes very obvious to the opponent where the ball is.   The quarterback should be standing rather tall when he releases the ball, since this tends to send it on a direct route to the receiver.   If the man is crouched low, the ball will arch and will be difficult to catch.

A few helpful hints that we have gathered on feeding the ball are brought in here for your perusal.   We tell our quarterbacks to treat the football as if it were a bubble.   When the back is coming in to take the ball, the quarterback should have it lying in his hand just like a big bubble.   As the runner approaches, a little split vision should be employed to see just where the pocket is, and the ball raised or lowered accordingly.   In players who have worked together often, this should never be necessary, but sometimes under game pressure it is required.   We do not want our quarterback to take so much as one peek at the ball carrier after the latter takes the ball.   Our instructions to the quarterback are, "Feed, fake, and flee."   That is, we ask him to hand off to the right halfback, fake hard to the left halfback, and then flee back to fake a forward pass.   Remember each one of these motions is separate from the other.   Do not allow a quarterback to try to combine them.   He should make certain that both hands are firmly on the ball when faking, because even an exceptional faker might lose the ball.

Too much stress cannot be put on this phase of our offense, and before practice starts we have our individual backfields work out with their center for as long as we possibly can allow them to do so.   The more familiar your quarterback becomes with his backfield teammates, the better precision you will have in your ball-handling department.   Have the halfbacks check the quarterback on his fakes and vice versa. Feeding the ball is exceedingly important, and we ask our quarterback always to keep in mind the height of the man who is going to get the ball on the next play. An exceptionally tall man in your backfield will make things a bit more complicated for your quarterback, but so long as he keeps his wits about him, he will have little or no trouble. A cool-headed quarterback can do more to keep the "T" running smoothly on Saturday afternoon than all the talk in the world.

QUARTERBACK'S PLAY MOTIONS

"43"

We should like to give a complete résumé of what we ask our quarterback to do on the plays we have described in the earlier part of the book. On play "43" we ask the quarterback to take the ball with his left foot forward. As soon as he gets it from the center we want him to pull it into his stomach and then start his reverse pivot. Once his left foot is placed solidly on the ground he should take one step off with his right foot and start feeding the ball to the right halfback. Once the ball carrier has passed, the quarterback should step out with his left foot and then once again with his right. It is at this time that the fake to the left halfback should commence. It is difficult to make your quarterback fake very hard at the start. A drill that we installed made faking just a routine matter, and we like it very much. What we do is to ask our left halfback to extend several of his fingers in the direction of the quarterback when the lateral is being faked to him. We then question our signal caller as to how many fingers he saw. This makes it imperative that the quarterback keep his eyes on the left halfback rather than the ball carrier. This little maneuver has done more to deceive the defense than any other backfield training device we have yet come across.   Have the backs take to this like a game —if they really enjoy doing it, they will do it correctly.

After the fake is made, the quarterback's left foot is about to hit the ground.   When this happens he should pivot on the ball of his left foot and start to run in the direction opposite that which the ball carrier is taking.   When he is running back he should keep his shoulders hunched over to conceal the pocket where the ball would be.   When he has reached a point about six yards behind the line of scrimmage he should execute an about face and fake a forward pass. While faking this pass he should study the entire situation to see just how the defensive team reacted to the play, and at what points they were weak.

"29H"

For our second play, number "29H," we have the identical movements.   The quarterback just "rides" the ball back into his stomach after faking to the right halfback, and when he steps out in the direction of the left half he actually has the ball, which he laterals to the number two back.

MOUSETRAP

On the mousetrap play we have the signal caller execute a reverse pivot and take one step out to fake to the fullback. Once that man is past, the quarterback takes one step and pivots all the way around so that he steps out parallel to the line of scrimmage.   Again he takes two steps before handing the ball off to the number two back.   This time he is handing off with his left leg forward rather than the right.   When the ball is released he steps down on his right foot and makes his pivot to go back and fake the pass.   We realize this is slightly repetitious, but we feel that it is well to correlate this material under both the play as a whole, and under the individual position.

FULLBACK LATERAL

On our fullback lateral play we ask our quarterback to perform his reverse pivot and immediately take two steps out and fake a lateral to the fullback. He should push the ball far out so that it can be seen, before he pivots around toward the number two back, who is faking a "21 trap." Work hard to deceive the enemy when pushing the ball into the left half's stomach. As the ball is drawn back, the right foot should be hitting the ground, so that a quick pivot can be made. The back should turn almost completely around, taking two steps before releasing the ball from the waist. This play requires a cool-headed quarterback because he spends quite a bit of time with the ball in his possession, and the general tendency is to rush things. Johnny Lujack performed admirably on this play in our Army game in 1947. He took ample time and made good fakes, which made it much easier for our fullback to get the jump on the defensive backs.

"67F"

On the "67F" play we have our quarterback's feet in exactly the opposite position; that is, the right foot forward. This allows him to perform a reverse pivot and end up just one step away from the spot where the end will come to take the ball from him. This simplifies the play a great deal, and we feel that on such a play it is not necessary to spend any extra time trying to deceive the opponent. It works rapidly, and looks so much like a fullback buck play that we do not like to have our quarterback draw anyone's attention to the fact that he did not hand off to the fullback.

"27F"

On the "27F" play we have the quarterback make a partial pivot and stop with his left foot placed so that he is in a position to fake hard to the fullback, who is coming in fast toward the center's left hip.   As soon as the fullback is past, he should force himself around the rest of the way by using his shoulder.   When his left foot strikes the ground for the second time he should take off at once with his right and be prepared to feed the ball to the left halfback immediately. This back will be cutting across very rapidly, and the quarterback will have to move swiftly.   When executed correctly, this play will warm the cockles of many a coach's heart.

PASSING—FOOTWORK

We have covered the art of passing from the throwing standpoint, and now we would like to spend a few moments on the quarterback's footwork when he is preparing to pass. On nearly every one of our pass plays we have the passer run back to a spot five or six yards behind the line of scrimmage before turning.   On an "11 pass" it will be five yards if the passer's left foot is forward when he receives the ball from the center, and six if his right foot is in front.   This comes about because if he steps off with his left foot after the reverse pivot is made, it will be six steps before he is in a position to make the second pivot correctly.   We ask our men to hit the ground hard with their right foot, and turn fast on the ball of that foot with a little help from the shoulder. As soon as they complete the pivot they should plant the left foot firmly on the ground and start looking for the potential receivers. All passes developing from our running plays will require the quarterback to perform the same tasks.

NOTRE DAME'S "T MASTERS"

A complete book could be written on how valuable a good quarterback is to the "T" formation. We do not want to elaborate to that extent, but we would like to relate a few incidents that have come up with our quarterbacks during recent seasons. We like to talk about our quarterbacks because we are exceptionally proud of them. In such young men as Angelo Bertelli, Johnny Lujack, George Ratterman, and Frank Tripucka we have had lads who will always be a distinct credit to football, to Notre Dame, and to whatever they do after they leave the ranks of professional football. These men possessed the character, the determination, and the fortitude to become outstanding in the position. None of them were "T Masters" when they came to Notre Dame, but I should be willing to match them against any quarterback in the business today.

Johnny Lujack was always a great opportunist, and always put team success far above his personal gain. Early in the season of 1947 our running attack just would not seem to function, with the result that it was necessary for Johnny to play the major role with his passing. As one Eastern sports writer put it after our game with Pittsburgh that year, "Notre Dame without Lujack's passing would be like a kite without a tail." He may have been correct at that time, but as the season rolled along, the running game sharpened up and we became a fairly potent organization on the ground. The Southern California game of that year was to be the last which John Lujack ever would play for Notre Dame. It would have been easy for John to call many passes and make himself stand out on the field that day. However, our running game was clicking perfectly, so John threw but two passes. Nevertheless, he was still outstanding; he intercepted one pass and ran it back forty-seven yards, and batted down another behind the goal line. This young man, who always put the team's success first, found that it paid him the highest possible dividends.

George Ratterman, who is one of four men ever to win four monograms in one year at Notre Dame, was indeed an amazing young gentleman and one who could always see a little humor in every situation. George was quarterbacking Notre Dame to victory in our 1946 game with Southern California, when suddenly one of his passes was intercepted. After coming off the field George was queried as to why he had thrown the ball so close to the defensive back. His answer was, "Why, coach, he was the only man open." George improved tremendously as that season progressed, being responsible for fifteen of the last nineteen touchdowns scored by our National Champions that year. Many men who have seen Buffalo play in the All America Conference tell me that Ratterman's faking has set innumerable backs free for long runs.

Frank Tripucka is fast coming into his own after having spent two years in the shadow of two of America's top "T" quarterbacks. Mechanically, "Trip" is a better quarterback than any we have ever coached, and we feel that after he gets one year of professional football under his belt he will go on to become one of the outstanding signal callers in the business. Frank came to Notre Dame as a seventeen year old boy, and I can truthfully say that I have never seen a lad who could absorb more knowledge than he, and demonstrate it on the football field.

There will always be a soft spot in my heart for Angelo Bertelli. He was the man around whom we built all of our hopes and dreams when we shifted into the "T" in 1942.

He more than lived up to our highest expectations as he led
Notre Dame to their many successful years in the "T," and
went on to become the first "T" quarterback ever to win the
Heisman Trophy.   Many are wont to place the blame of our
two defeats in 1942 on the fact that Angelo was not accustomed to handling the ball from the "T."   This is indeed an
error, because we honestly feel, without attempting to alibi
in any way, that if injuries to vital men such as Gerry Cowhig,
Dippy Evans, Creighton Miller, Walter Ziemba, and Lou
Rymkus had not occurred in 1942, we would have had one
of our most successful seasons.   All of the above mentioned
players had proved, and did prove later, that they were outstanding men on the football field.   Whenever I think of
Angelo Bertelli I think of the greatest passer in football.

12

Halfback and Fullback Play

ONCE AGAIN, it is *desire* that we look for first when we are selecting our ball carriers. During the course of a game this quality is outwardly tested in these men more than it is in the linemen. How many times have you seen a good back surrounded by a wall of tacklers, and before you know how or why, he is free again? Instruct your ball carriers to think always in terms of not being tackled and never being stopped until the whistle blows.

Relaxation is a very important requisite in a ball carrier. His timing has to be gauged to the split second, and he must be at ease when he receives the ball because in running at such a high speed, it is very easy for him to fumble.

BALL HANDLING

When instructing our ball carriers on the fundamentals, the first thing we ask them to do is to make certain that their hand nearest the quarterback is down when they receive the ball. I am not trying to say that this is the only way, but we have found that it has reduced the number of fumbles by a considerable amount. This has also helped out with the timing. We ask our backs to come in and take a slight peek at the ball, snatch it, seize it, tuck it away, and move it down-field. The main advantage of the ball carrier having his inside hand back develops when your quarterback has made his spin a little slower than usual. If the ball carrier had his hands out to reach for the ball, he would be past the quarter-back before the ball arrived. By having his inside hand down, the back has formed a pocket that will remain available to the quarterback until the runner is almost up to the line of scrimmage. I believe you will find this situation coming up many times, due either to a slow-spinning quarterback or an exceptionally fast-starting halfback.

Our halfbacks and fullbacks line up with one foot slightly back, the hands on the knees. The reason for our requiring that the one foot be back is to avoid their taking a false step backward before starting in the direction of the goal line. Invariably a boy will take one step backward before he starts to run, unless he has one foot back to begin with. You may be thinking, "All these details don't mean much." True, as individual details they are minor in scope, but we find that if you include countless details in one simple play, it makes the difference between a good play and a great one.

The ball carrier's inside leg should always be on its backward stride when he receives the ball; that is, the hip on which he receives the ball should never be coming forward. A good back with the right kind of knee action is very likely to knock the ball out of the quarterback's hands if he comes in with the inside leg moving forward.

On the first day of spring practice we line up our ball carriers and have them take the ball from the quarterback just as they would on a quick-opening play. However, we ask them to take the ball in only one hand, and that is the inside hand. They keep running in and taking the ball in the one hand until they have completely mastered this maneuver. Spend as much time as you can on this early in the practice sessions, since you will not want to waste time on it when the boys start to shape up physically. We would suggest that you have them perform this exercise for thirty minutes every day until they have it down to perfection. You will be amazed at the expressions that come over the faces of the young lads when they realize that they can master the art of taking the ball in one hand. It pleases them a great deal.

Success will result if they can just learn to control that hand and keep it there, and then run their stomach right into the ball. Have your men stand tall when they come in to get the ball. An expression that we have used thousands of times is, "Come in taller." If they will do this, I do not see how a fumble can occur at the time the ball is changing hands.

Then, after a while, after your boys have mastered the trick of coming in and taking the ball in the one hand, the next phase of the training consists of taking the ball in both hands. As soon as the man gets both hands on the pigskin he tucks it under one arm or the other. (See the photo of Larry Coutre receiving the ball following page 132.)

PLAY ROUTINES FOR BALL CARRIERS

Now that we have the receiving fundamentals understood, we would like to review each minute detail of the motions of the backs on the plays we have outlined in the earlier part of the book.

"43"

On play number "43" our right halfback should step out with his left foot; then as his right leg is stretching out the ball should be coming in to him on his left side. Once the ball is his, he should run straight into the hole. We ask our backs always to run fairly tall. If the holes are not opening up fast enough for a tall man to make his way, we let our tackles and guards try to run through these small holes a few times. Soon after that, the holes seem to open up much better. Once through the hole, the ball carrier is on his own, although we do ask him to cut to his left if that would be a prudent move.

The fullback steps out on this play with his right foot and swings wide around the right end, while the left halfback is faking hard.   As soon as the ball is snapped the left half should step out at full speed with his right foot and run hard until he is directly behind the quarterback, at which spot he should start to "belly" back until he reaches a point about seven yards behind the line of scrimmage.

"29H"

On the "29H" play the maneuvers are the same but, of course, the number four back does not receive the ball.   Instead he should hunch up his right shoulder and double over a little to conceal the pocket as he hits the line just as hard as if he were carrying the ball.   We instruct our left halfback to follow the same routine on faking that we give to our quarterback.   We ask him to tell us how many fingers the quarterback extends when he fakes this play.   Then when the "real McCoy" is called, the left halfback will be doing exactly the same thing as he did on the "43."

One thing that we require of all our backs and linemen is to step off on the foot that is nearest the direction in which they will be moving.   This is the most natural thing in the world, but you will find many backs who want to cross over with their other leg.   Ninety-nine out of one hundred persons will step off in the proper manner on the street, but get a lad on the football field and he wants to do it the hard way. Drill the men on this, since it is a time-saver when things are going rough.

Ask your backs to spend some of their spare time thinking up little faking maneuvers that will throw the opposing linemen off guard.   Whenever a back notices one of the enemy linemen looking through the line, he should strive diligently to give that man the wrong impression as to where the play is going.   This may be accomplished by staring directly at a certain hole, or by pointing a foot in a certain direction. If our man is not the intended ball carrier, then he may wet his hands or make any such move that might be made by a man contemplating reception of the pigskin.

ASSIGNING PLAYERS TO POSITIONS

If ever it were possible to have perfect backfield material, you would be wise to follow the ensuing suggestions as to assignment of positions. With both a right-handed and a left-handed passer, the former should run from the left halfback slot and the latter from the right halfback position. With two punters in the backfield, one should run from full-back to give you a man in position for a quick kick when needed. Naturally, any coach who ever found such material would no doubt die of heart failure, but in our many pleasant dreams we have seen ourselves sitting on the bench with a backfield of the aforementioned caliber performing before a packed house every Saturday afternoon. Even though you may seldom use your halfbacks as passers, it is ideal to have one who is capable of throwing the ball, since he will be a constant threat to the opponent. A quick-kicking fullback will help out many times. We have found that a thirty-five yard quick kick sometimes bears more fruit than a sixty yard planned punt—especially when kicking to such a gentleman as Buddy Young of Illinois.

Large size is not a prime requisite in a halfback. On our 1947 squad Emil Sitko was our heaviest halfback, and his playing weight was about 176 pounds. If you have a fair-sized line and your backs are willing to hustle for sixty minutes, you will find yourself doing quite well on the score-board. Instruct your small backs to spend as much time as possible on their speed, especially when starting from an upright position. Speed is an asset which will make up for size in the backfield.

BLOCKING

It is very seldom that we ask our backs to do much blocking, principally because of their physical stature. However, when we do desire them to block, we want them to do it correctly. Quite often an intelligent back can outsmart a hard-charging lineman if he really works at it. When the opponent is coming in speedily, he is susceptible to almost any kind of a fake. If the back will fake very hard with his head to one side of the enemy and then block for all he is worth on the other side before the opponent regains his poise, he should be able to remove him from the play. When we ask our fullback to block on pass plays we like to have him remain on his feet as long as possible. This makes it somewhat more difficult for him, but if he will keep going down with the man, he will be able to scuffle long enough for the passer to release the ball. We like to see our fullbacks down on all fours and still charging ahead into the opposing end.

BACKFIELD DEFENSE

We will cover in this chapter, the assignments of all four backs for the times when the opponent has the ball, rather than separating the quarterback's duties. The reason for this is that today, with so many defensive specialists in the game, we no longer have definite positions as such. We list our defensive positions as the linebackers, the halfbacks, and the safety man. Many teams today shift their men completely around on defense. The Chicago Cardinals use their outstanding end, Mal Kutner, as a defensive halfback because of his "ball-hawking" ability. During 1946 and 1947 we used Russ Ashbaugh at every position in our backfield while on defense.

For clarity's sake we will give the assignments as we use

them when we have the best material at all positions. Our left-side linebacker is our fullback. The center linebacker is our right guard, with our center filling in the linebacker's hole on the right. If we shift into a six-man line, the guard jumps up into this last position. Our two halfbacks play the defensive spots as shown in all of the plays we have diagrammed, with the safety position being filled by the quarterback.

The fullback's duty is to watch closely all of the movements of the opposing right end and right tackle. That is his zone, and he is held responsible for it. We do not want him to leave it unguarded until he is absolutely certain that the play will not come through that space. He should move like a cat at all times—going either to his right or left, but always being ready to spring after the ball carrier when he sees an opening for a definite move. He should never allow a back to run outside of his end. His job is to drive the ball carrier in toward his teammates if it is impossible for him to make the tackle himself. On passes he should watch the left-hand flat and be on the lookout for something similar to our own "angle right" pass.

The distance away from the line that the halfbacks play is determined by the situation. On a small yardage situation they should play up rather close to the line, moving back on each play that increases the distance that the opponents must gain to reach their objective. They should never allow a man to get behind them, nor should they ever leave their zone when a pass is in the offing. When they are absolutely certain that the enemy is going to run the ball, the halfbacks should sprint up and aid in the tackling. A halfback can be especially helpful on end sweeps because usually he is just about as tricky as the ball carrier and it is easier for him to bring this man down in the open. A chapter is devoted to the defensive activities of the backs on passes, so we shall discuss only the running game in this section.

The safety man is your last chance to guard your goal line. It is he who should be capable of diagnosing the plays as soon as they start to operate. As soon as he "dopes out" a play he should inform all of his teammates and start taking immediate measures to halt the proceedings. The safety man has a very fine vantage point from which to see what is going on, and as soon as he sees the hole open up and the ball carrier headed toward it with the ball tucked under his arm, he should bolt right up and make the tackle. When facing a "sharp" "T" outfit, you will find that a great many of your tackles will have to be made by your safety man. This is brought about by the split second timing that makes it possible for the opponent to hold even the greatest line-men out long enough for the back to get through the hole. Whenever a coach is fortunate enough to have two defensive safety men such as Russ Ashbaugh and Johnny Lujack on the same squad, he does not have to lose any sleep over the possibility of enemy runners going the distance. These two young men were great on defense because they loved to play it. They got every bit as much enjoyment out of making a good, solid tackle as they did in scoring six points.

GROUP WORK

When we have our backfield men congregate at the start of practice for their individual group work, we have them follow this procedure. All of the quarterbacks gather to-gether with the centers and practice at the same time. Each of the quarterbacks should call out the signals simultane-ously. This will get them all in the habit of using the same cadence, thus making it much easier for the center and the backs who have to take the ball on the run.

The shoulder drop is one of the fullback's most potent weapons, and we try to have them develop this little trick. At the start of practice we have all of our fullbacks gather at the tackling dummy. We have our backfield coach stand outside of the pit as if he were the quarterback, and he feeds the ball to the fullback as the latter rushes in. When the back gets to the dummy he drops his shoulder and hits the dummy very hard. You will find that if your men work at this long enough they will begin to like it. It will prove an invaluable asset when a fullback meets a linebacker and a few yards are desperately needed.

The halfbacks should work daily on their starts. A big fault which we find is that backs are able to start quickly on a one or two count, but when the quarterback runs plays on a different count in a game, they either jump the gun or are too late. In practice have them run on every count from one to five. Change the count continually so they will pay particular attention to on what number the play is being run. A little off-season work with the track team may help immeasurably in speeding up their starts and controlling their jumpiness.

Just before organizing your scrimmage, line up three or four backfields that you plan to use and let them run up and down the field together, running almost all of the basic plays. This will acquaint them with the movements of their teammates. Be patient with your backs; theirs is a task which takes long, hard hours of work, but one that will pay off extremely large dividends.

13

End Play

END PLAY in this modern era of football requires more each year from the aspirants for this all-important position. The end of today must be classified as a semi-lineman and semi-back, since at times he is called upon to perform duties familiar to both these positions. In order to be a great end, a lad must excel in blocking, tackling, receiving passes, carrying the ball, covering punts, and also should be one of the first to analyze each and every play. Speed, agility, strength, and endurance, along with height and weight will better equip the end for the tasks he is called upon to perform. It is seldom that you run across a man with all of these characteristics, and we have found that most of the truly great ends have made up in *desire* what they lack in the natural assets.

THE END ON OFFENSE

The end on offense must be an excellent blocker. His line blocking is much more difficult to perform than that of the other linemen. The reasons for this are: first, the end is facing the toughest defensive lineman, the tackle; second, his blocks must be held longer than those applied by the men in the middle of the line; and third, his target is farther away from him on the "Down" signal. Many of his line blocks are actually semi open field blocks, and we have found that two out of every three blocks a "T" end makes must be open field maneuvers. The coach who can develop good open field blocking in the end department will have a very successful "T" formation.

With the continuing importance of the passing game in football, the ability to catch passes has become the second most important phase of offensive end play. There is not a "T" team in the country today that does not spend a great deal of time on the perfection of its passing game. Also of great importance to the end on offense is his ability to cover on punts. Many of the old school still like to place this ahead of pass receiving in importance, but we feel that since the pass occurs so many more times in a game than does the kick, we prefer to spend more time on the development of good receivers. The fourth requisite of a good end is that he must be able to run with the ball. The end around play is being used more each year, and a good end can make this a great play. The ball-carrying end must learn the arts of the fake, the stiff-arm, dodging, and how to make use of his blockers. The fifth trait we look for in an end candidate is that he be an actor. Ever so many times during the course of a game he is called upon to run as a decoy, and if he carries out that duty to perfection, he will save a great deal of wear and tear on the other members of the team.

BLOCKING

Stance.—Our ends have been told that we think the best blocking stance is the tripod position; that is, with one hand resting on the ground and the feet parallel to each other. Some men can charge faster if one foot is placed slightly behind the other. The shoulders should be square with the line of scrimmage and each the same distance from the ground. The hips should be slightly lower than the shoulders; the back must be firm and fairly straight. We insist that the head be up and the neck "bulled." The free forearm rests on the adjacent knee. We teach this stance because we feel that from it the lineman can start to his left, his right, or forward with equal speed and agility. (See photo of Jim Martin illustrating this stance following page 132.)

The normal location of the end in the "T" formation is one yard out from the offensive tackle. On any play where the end is not concerned with the actual running of the play, he should vary his position in a manner that will help conceal his intentions on the important plays. When the quarterback calls "End out," it means that the end moves out to a spot ten yards away from his offensive tackle.

Charging.—The art of charging must be mastered if the end is to get over fast enough to block the opponent. Most common for end play is the "step-in" charge, in which the entire body moves into the opponent with the initial step forward, contact with the shoulder being made at the completion of the number one step. In view of the importance of "step-in" blocking, we have outlined the principles that must be adhered to in order to achieve success in this most important operation. First, in man-for-man blocking the initial step is taken with the foot that is nearer the ultimate target. That is, in blocking an opponent to the right, step first with the right foot, and vice versa for a block to the left. Second, in double team blocking the post blocker takes his initial step with the foot opposite the direction of the block, while the pressure blocker steps out with the foot nearest the target. At the completion of the charge the feet should be well spread and occupying a position well under the blocker's body.

Good blocking, which is the essence of offensive football, results from aggressive determined effort and desire on every play plus perfection of the mechanics. The mechanics of good blocking are: (1) head up, (2) bull neck, (3) eyes on target, (4) back straight, (5) weight concentrated on balls of feet, (6) feet widespread, (7) forearm up close to body, and (8) body control.

Shoulder Block.—This is the number one weapon of the

offensive wingman. It allows him to keep his feet and be of further use to the ball carrier after the initial block is performed. First we have the straight shoulder block, which is executed from a tripod stance. The end drives forward with a well-controlled, low, hard charge, aiming for the thigh of the opponent. He must govern his charge so that he will be at his maximum momentum when the contact is made, and so that his body will be braced to meet the shock of the impact. The initial contact is made with the opponent's thigh, and as the blocker takes his short, digging steps, he slides his shoulder on up toward the midsection of the target. As he comes up, he should raise the arm of the blocking shoulder so that the elbow is up to shoulder level, thus giving him more with which to block. The free hand may be dropped to the ground for support if necessary. When applying a straight shoulder block in the open field, the end should get close to his target and then coil himself to perform all of the maneuvers as if he were at the line of scrimmage. It is essential that open field blocks be made with speed, but not without body control. Just before the contact the blocker should slow down enough to secure body balance and control. In the use of any shoulder block the importance of moving the enemy laterally cannot be overemphasized. It is much more desirable to move an opponent one yard laterally than it is to drive him back four yards. A shoulder blocker should aim his head at the midsection of the enemy, and as the contact is made, he should pull his head away and let the shoulder take the impact. This will keep his head on the target all the way and make it extremely difficult for the enemy to fake him out.

Reverse Shoulder Block.—This is the second maneuver we teach our ends on offense. In this operation our end approaches the enemy as if he were going to apply a straight shoulder block, but just before contact is made he reverses and hits the enemy with the opposite shoulder. This block is used frequently against slicing linemen or against men who have penetrated too deeply into our backfield. The end's shoulder should hit the target just below the midsection and should slide up a little as leverage is gained. All other shoulder blocks are slight variations of the two mentioned, and should not be employed unless, owing to the size of your personnel, it is imprudent to use the aforementioned methods.

Body Block.—This block does not play such an important part in the play of offensive ends, but they must know the fundamentals of this maneuver in order to vary their tactics. First, we teach the cross body block, which is executed either from a stationary or a running position. The end comes close enough to apply a shoulder block, drops his shoulder, and throws his body above the knees and across the thighs of the defender. The contact is made with the blocker's hip; his arms are straight, his head up, back straight, and the inside knee raised a little. This type of block should not be applied in the open field when the opponent is moving straight at the blocker, but rather when the potential tackler is coming in from the side.

Reverse Body Block.—The reverse body block is executed with the same deception as the reverse shoulder block. The end uses this block mainly to remove the far linebacker on trap plays. As soon as the end reverses his position, he lets his body fly at the thighs of the enemy. The third body block is what we have named the long block. It is executed from a running position by throwing the body across the knees of the enemy in an attempt to cut his legs out from under him. Contact is made with the hip, and is followed up with a rolling motion. The long body block requires perfect timing and position, and should be used widely in open field blocking.

Blocking Linemen.—Since the main task of an offensive end is to block the defensive tackle, we have outlined a few steps to combat the various types of charges the tackle is likely to use. When the end faces a "straight hard shoulder charge," he should meet the enemy with a straight shoulder block by taking the initial step in the direction toward which he plans to drive the man. If the enemy is more than one foot away at the completion of the first step, the end should switch and hit him with a reverse shoulder block. If he tries the straight block from that distance, he will find the opponent slipping away. Against a "slicing charge" the reverse shoulder block should be employed. This is a difficult block, which must be perfected if the off tackle play is going to work successfully. If the enemy goes into a "high retreating charge," the end should employ a high, knifelike, straight shoulder block, keeping his feet and applying hard, steady pressure. The "waiting forearm shiver charge" is combated with a fierce shoulder block and the use of the head fake to throw the enemy's arms out of the path.

Blocking Linebackers.—In blocking linebackers, the body blocks are usually the most effective. We prefer to have our ends employ this method on linebackers because it keeps the enemy out of the play longer than does the shoulder block. Downfield blocking calls for use of the shoulder block, cross body block, and the long body block. The latter two are most common in this situation because we definitely want the opponent taken out of the path of the ball carrier. If there is more than one blocker with the runner, we prefer the body block, whereas one blocker against many potential tacklers might make a shoulder block more feasible.

Protecting the Kicker.—The end is not looked upon as primarily a protector of the punter, but under certain conditions he is an important factor in this task. On a team with a right-footed kicker, the left end must always give attention to the matter of protection before covering the kick. When he assumes his position he must make certain that the defensive end cannot line up inside of him. As the ball is snapped, he should check the defending wingman with a severe shoulder block before going down under the kick. If the defensive end is more than three yards outside of him, it is not required that our man waste any time with him. In blocking for a field goal or extra point attempt, the end lines up close to the offensive tackle and uses an aggressive check block to prevent the enemy from crashing.

PASS RECEIVING

Catching forward passes is one of the more important functions of end play. Although pass receiving skill must to a large extent be natural ability, the end will find that it is possible to become great at this phase by spending his time on practicing the correct technique.

Running Out.—In getting into position to receive a forward pass, the end must first clear the line of scrimmage immediately. He must avoid tipping off the play, yet keep away from the enemy as much as possible. When a pass is likely, the opponents are quite apt to try to "jam" the end as he attempts to get clear. If such is the case, he must trick them into thinking that he is going to block the tackle by giving him a good, solid head fake. As the man reacts to the fake, the end should be on his way. Once through the line, the end should try to steer clear of the linebacker if at all possible. If this defender comes at him, the end should feint a shoulder block and side-step the enemy.

The Catch.—Passes should be caught just with the hands whenever possible, with no effort to use the arms or body as aids in holding the ball. The hands and wrists should be loose and relaxed, with the fingers spread comfortably wide. The receiver must keep his eye on the forward point of the ball after he has committed himself and is about ready to make the catch. His concentration on the ball must be so intent that a violent impact or blow will not cause his vision to waver from the pigskin or affect his determination to catch it. As the ball approaches the end, his strides should be short if possible. This will avoid jolting of the head. Many receivers like to leave the ground in one long step so as to avoid this jolting when the ball arrives.

In general, passes above the chest should be caught with the thumbs pointing in, whereas passes below the chest should be received with the thumbs pointing out. There is one exception to this rule, which arises when the ball is being taken over the shoulder. At this time the thumbs should be pointing out. As the ball touches the hands they should give slightly, much in the manner of the hands of a baseball player catching a hard line drive. The receiver should not extend his hands until he is in a position to make the catch.

Getting Free.—The ability to get free of the defenders is every bit as important as the ability to catch the ball. Many of the older pass catchers are experts at this art. Such men as Ken Kavanaugh, Mal Kutner, and Billy Dewell have perfected this phase of pass catching and are frequently in the open when the ball arrives. Various methods are used to shake loose from the defensive backs. Some of the most important tricks are: First, the fake-and-break method, in which the end runs directly for the defender, feints his body and head sharply in one direction, and cuts away to the opposite side. Second is the buttonhook, which calls for the receiver to start down the field as if he were on his way to receive a long pass. Instead he stops suddenly and turns to face the passer while a bullet pass is approaching. Third, the spin is executed much like the buttonhook, except that the pass receiver pivots in the air. That is, he jumps high and turns to face the passer. Fourth, we have our men work hard at developing a change of pace. In this maneuver the runner puts on a pretense of running at full speed but keeps a considerable burst of energy in reserve, and just as the defender turns to keep pace the receiver taps the reserve.

Decoys.—One of the most important and at the same time one of the most neglected phases of the passing game is the work of the decoys. A good decoy should actually imagine that the quarterback may possibly throw the ball to him, and in this way he should display all of the mannerisms that he employs when going out to receive a pass. He must realize that unless he and every other decoy compel at least one man to follow them the play will in all probability fail. A decoy who does not look back for the pass is wasting time and energy. When running as a decoy the receiver should observe carefully how the opponents are covering him and report accordingly to the signal caller. He should try his various fakes against the defenders when decoying to see how they react to them.

COVERING KICKS

In punt formation the normal location of the ends is as follows: The *left end* should be about three yards out from the offensive tackle. His first job is to see that the defensive end stays outside of him, and if he can spread as far as four yards and still keep the end outside of him, then we like him to do so. Unless the opposing end is out at least four yards from our tackle, our man must check block him for two counts. Second, the *right end* should be spread wide outside of the opposing left end. As a rule, the end will find it to his advantage to run directly at the defending left halfback. This will keep the play to his left and enable him to make his move toward the ball when necessary. He should always keep the play inside and make the ball carrier run into a zone that is properly patrolled. The end should not look back until he hears the thud of the kick, at which time a quick glance over his shoulder will be sufficient to inform him of the approximate path of the ball.   Usually the end will be able to determine the position of the ball by observing the man who is preparing to make the catch.

DEFENSIVE END PLAY

The responsibilities of the end on defense are summarized as follows: First, he must force the runner to cut in toward the line of scrimmage.   Second, on a sweep he must drive the runner deep behind the line of scrimmage so that the linebacker can come up and make the tackle before the ball carrier reaches the line.   Third, he must strip the runner of all of his interference.   Fourth, on extremely wide plays he must force the runner out of bounds before he allows him to cut up the field.   Fifth, he should tackle the runner before he gets to the line if there are no blockers.   The defensive stance of individual ends varies with the man, and we find that the players know best how they can operate at top efficiency.   Therefore we let them govern themselves accordingly.   (Following page 132 is a photo of the defensive stance employed by right end Leon Hart of Notre Dame.)   The end's location should be as close to the defensive tackle as he can get without leaving himself vulnerable to a block from the outside.

TYPE OF PLAY

In our opinion, the most effective, as well as the most difficult, type of end play is the smash and drift technique.   This method has the end crash to meet the off tackle plays and drift when a wide play is formulating.   In the execution of this type of defensive play, the end makes an initial charge of three steps—the first being with his right foot.   The length and spread of these steps varies with the time it takes the opposing blockers to reach our man. In stopping off tackle plays, he must be ready to meet pressure at the conclusion of his third step, at which time his outside foot should be to the rear. From this position he must drive low with his shoulder into the interference. In countering a wide play, after meeting the reaction point (one to three steps, depending upon when he sizes up the attack) the end shuttles outward, using hands, forearms, and clever footwork to keep the opponents from his body. The secret of success in using this type of defensive end play is the development of the reaction reflex. Experience is the only means of developing extraordinary reflexes along these lines. Spend as much time as possible on full-speed defensive drills. Trial and error has convinced us that the smash and drift technique is the best type of defensive end play.

RUSHING THE PASSER AND KICKER

The pass defense of a team depends heavily on the ability of the ends effectively to rush the passer. It is imperative that they rush without opening the way for running plays on fake passes. The end must avoid extremes when rushing. He should go outside of the blockers to get at the passer. Should the blocker be playing exceptionally wide, the end should feint at him and cut inside.

When opposing a punt formation the end should be cautious in rushing unless it is a sure kicking situation. If he is uncertain, he should retard the opposing end at the line of scrimmage while he diagnoses the play. When the end does rush the kicker, he must move quickly and along the shortest path to the spot where the kicker's foot will meet the ball. He should leave his feet in a high diving attempt to clutch the ball as it leaves the opponent's foot.

COMMON DEFENSIVE ERRORS

When our ends are making mistakes on defense, we can usually attribute the error to one of the following:

1. Charging too deep on the initial charge.
2. Meeting blockers in an upright position.
3. Wrong initial step.
4. Retreating ahead of runner in attempt to get around the blocker.
5. Not enough penetration on initial charge.
6. Failure to use hands on blocker.
7. Chasing ball carrier on plays to opposite flank; the end should cut behind line of scrimmage.
8. Failure to use shoulder and elbow in meeting off tackle plays.
9. Disregarding close flanker.
10. Favoring defense to outside, with resultant gains being made inside the end.

When an end has overcome the above faults, you will find you have a great wingman.

14

Tackle and Guard Play

IN VIEW OF THE FACT that these two positions have so much in common, we are going to cover them in the same chapter. As previously mentioned, the guard lines up eight inches from the center, while the tackle locates himself one foot out from the guard. (Following page 132 are photos of left tackle George Connor, right tackle Zig Czarobski, left guard Bill Fischer, and right guard Marty Wendell, illustrating correct offensive and defensive stances for their positions.)

OFFENSIVE CHARGING AND BLOCKING

The "step-in charge" is advocated for general use by these linemen. In its execution the entire body is in contact with the enemy at the conclusion of the initial step. It is imperative that the foot that is in front and the full body charge be moving together in a straight line in order to obtain maximum impact-momentum. It is important to notice also that the initial step in the line blocking must carry the blocker to a point where he can intercept the charge of the defender, absorb his shock, and still be able to follow through with his movement. The same types of blocks as given to the ends are taught to our tackles. That is, the straight shoulder block, the reverse shoulder block, the cross body block, the reverse body block, and the long body block. These linemen do not have as much use for the body blocks as do the ends, but since we require our offside linemen to do considerable downfield blocking, we want them to have this art down to perfection.

167

TRAPPING

Mousetrapping a guard or a tackle requires speed and perfect body control.   In a trapping assignment the blocker should anticipate finding his target in the most difficult location, which of course would be in the hole.   He should be prepared to turn through the line and rout him out with a driving shoulder block.   Normally, however, the trapped lineman will be across the line of scrimmage, in which case the blocker should employ a shoulder swipe block, which would drive the man toward the sideline.   If the trapped lineman has penetrated deep into the backfield, a reverse shoulder block, or even a reverse body block, may be used.   Speed is of the utmost importance in trap blocking, but body control must not be sacrificed.

PASS PROTECTION

Interior linemen should never charge on pass plays.   Their main purpose is to protect the passer and not to block any particular opponent.   Another important reason is that the rules prohibit the presence of interior linemen in the defensive backfield during the execution of a forward pass.   To protect the passer, it is advisable for the blockers to have inside positions so that they may force the opponents to take the outside path to the passer.   The blocker should use the shoulder block to stop the enemy's charge.   If he continues to come in, a low body block should be thrown to stop his advance.   Should the defensive man be playing head on with the blocker, our man should step toward the center when the ball is snapped, thus forcing the enemy to go outside of him.

When this is accomplished he should pivot and bury his shoulder in the adversary.

PUNT PROTECTION

In protecting the kicker, the lineman is wholly and absolutely responsible for the area in front of him and the gap to his inside. In closing this seam he should never charge laterally, for in so doing he opens a space to his other side. The shoulder block is most generally used on this play, and much emphasis should be placed on the fact that the head must be kept up. Linemen should not give ground in kick protection but should strive for solid contact from a stationary position. Caution these men not to narrow the width of their base or turn their shoulders with the enemy. The length of time these blocks should be held depends upon the kicker; however, two full seconds should be long enough. As soon as they release their blocks the linemen should "fly" downfield to get into the fracas.

PULLING OUT OF THE LINE

Since it is not natural for a lineman to back out of position with great speed and body control, it requires long and arduous practice drills for him to master this very important fundamental of line play. In pulling out of the line to the right, the lineman pushes hard with the hand resting on the ground (tripod stance), and without raising up, turns rapidly to the right, pivoting on his right foot on an angle of about 100 degrees. At the same time he crosses over with his left foot to a point slightly behind and to the right of the original position of the right foot. When he starts to move out he should run parallel to the line of scrimmage. As soon as the pivot is complete he should be coiled and ready to strike. After reaching this position the lineman should strive diligently to pick up speed and momentum with each step, so that he may be as powerful as possible when he meets his target. Pulling linemen must be very careful not to tip off their plans. It is only natural that they tend to move one leg back a bit as they line up, but to do this is to waste the combined efforts of eleven men. Our pulling linemen always cross over toward the foot that is behind; that is, if they are going to the right, their right foot is behind when crossing over. When assigned to block the secondary on a "pull" play, we ask our linemen to muster all of the speed at their command as they drive into the gap where the play will be run. If they should meet any other opponent in that gap, they must forget all future responsibilities and make certain that they drive this opponent out of the attack zone. When they reach the secondary we like to have them take the backer-up with a shoulder block; however, if he is moving laterally toward the ball carrier, it may be necessary to apply a long body block. We ask our men to stay on their feet as long as possible; once they leave them, they are of no further use to the man with the ball.

DEFENSIVE PLAY

STANCE

There are three fundamental types of defensive stance. The first two can be used by either the guard or the tackle, whereas the third is for tackles only. The first is the four point stance, which is likened to a sprinter's start, with the exception of the weight balance and the wide base of the feet and hands. In this stance the back is straight and parallel to the ground, the weight is concentrated well forward, and the head is up. Usually one foot is slightly behind the other, depending on the shoulder to be used in contact. This stance provides maximum solidity and tremendous drive forward. Lateral movement from this stance is effective in rushing the passer or kicker. Second, we have the three point stance, which is similar to the offensive tripod stance. On defense we have the feet spread wider and more weight concentrated forward. The hips should be just slightly lower than the shoulders. Be careful that the buttocks does not get too low or the man will be pushed over easily. This stance is generally recognized as the best over-all position for general defensive line play. Although it does not permit the lineman to go as low as does the four point stance, it provides an effective charge forward and still maintains mobility to either side. It combines agility and power. Third is the crouch stance, which is an upright stance that we give only to our tackles. The body is crouched, knees bent, arms extended out in front and slightly bent at the elbow, weight evenly distributed, and feet either staggered or square. This stance provides a minimum of power forward and gives blockers relatively easy access to the body. Very little penetration is possible from this stance; however, it does permit excellent play vision and, consequently, diagnosis. This method is very effective for holding up ends and when facing mouse-trap plays. Generally, large rugged tackles are found using this stance for general game use. It is a big man's position.

The location of the defensive linemen is generally fixed by pre-game defensive plans. We like to have our linemen play as wide as they can and still be master of the territory between themselves and the men adjacent to them.

TACKLES ON DEFENSE

Defensive tackles are generally classed either as "charging" or "waiting" tackles. The charging tackle's main objective is to drive across the line of scrimmage in a low forceful movement, striving either to tackle the runner or strip him of his interference. In this drive the tackle attempts to break the charge of the blocker by means of superior speed and power transmitted through low shoulder, forearm, and hand contact. He must keep the blockers away from his legs, and fight through, not around, interference. Perhaps the most important movement in the initial charge of the tackle is his ability to react to the snap from the center. The tackle should be prepared to move as the ball is passed. He should concentrate on the movement of the ball through split vision. This initial charge must be made for the purpose of wholly overcoming the opponent and then recovering immediately to control possible resistance from another angle. The secret of success in a powerful initial charge is for the rear leg to be coming forward at the same time contact is being made with the shoulder. This maneuver gives maximum momentum to the charge.

The waiting tackle may operate from either a three point or a crouched stance. His main objective is to let the opponents declare themselves; through the use of strength and clever hand and footwork he maneuvers himself into an effective defensive position. This type of tackle play usually requires size and strength plus almost perfect coördination of hands and feet. A tackle who has mastered this technique is difficult to power block, but is less effective in rushing the passer. He seldom is able to strip interference from the runner because his initial charge carries no penetration.

The ideal situation exists when a coach has one charging

and one waiting tackle. We were fortunate enough to have such men during our 1946 and 1947 seasons. In George Connor we had a man who loved to burst in and upset the offensive applecart, whereas Zig Czarobski was a man who preferred to wait and stop anything that came his way. It is our firm belief that it was the combined actions of these two men that made both of them All Americans. When we opposed a team that liked to trap the tackles they were able to make George "bite," but Zig would pull over fast to close the gap. On the other hand, when we met a passing team or a team that spent considerable time on backfield maneuvers, George was usually in fast enough to break up their plans. Tackles will be either "chargers" or "waiters" by nature, and it is best to capitalize on their natural tendencies.

The defensive tackle uses two charges that are relatively easy to master. The first is the straight shoulder charge, which is most effective when employed from a three point stance. The second is the forearm shiver charge, which is especially useful when playing a single blocker. This charge is quite common against a "T" offense, whereas the straight shoulder charge is employed more often against "two on one" blocking set-ups. In the latter, the tackle contacts the opponent's shoulders with the palms of his hands, arms stiff. He brings his rear leg forward at the instant contact is made. From this position the tackle may hold the blocker at bay, he may straighten him up, drive him backward, or throw him to the right or left as he drifts to meet the play. This charge is excellent in long yardage situations; however, it gives the tackle a poor start if he plans on rushing the passer.

GUARDS ON DEFENSE

Guards should always employ a low stance on defense—that is, lower than the tackles. As the guard waits for each play, he should eye the ball with split vision. As soon as it is snapped he should start moving. We give our guards various defensive maneuvers, the first of these being the forearm shiver, which is carried out in the same manner as we outlined for the tackles. Second is the submarine charge, which is used on short yardage situations. It is a charge underneath the immediate opponent. As the ball is snapped, the guard charges straight forward with neck rigid, and making sure he gets his head under the opponent's knees. He must keep his eyes open and try to trip up the opposing lineman as he goes under. The most important phase of this charge is the quick recovery of balance and control by drawing the feet well up under the body and lifting the head and shoulders as soon as possible. At the conclusion of the charge the lineman should have the feet, knees, and hands on the ground and the head up, ready to make a driving, head-on tackle or to proceed forward and rush the passer. The feint and step charge consists of the man taking one step and pulling that leg back immediately. As soon as the opponent goes for that leg the guard should step in with the other. This feinting or drifting is very good on long yardage situations, since it allows the man to get up to the line but not much farther. The straight shoulder charge is best executed from the four point stance in the middle of the line. This gives maximum power and drive from a well-balanced start. The wide base should be kept throughout the charge, and the guard should take short, choppy steps to insure himself of solid footing. The object of this charge is to drive through the opponent and across the line of scrimmage. The secret is to bring the rear foot forward at the time the contact is being made with the shoulder and elbow. Have your guards vary their tactics as frequently as possible and they will find the going much easier.

HINTS ON GUARD AND TACKLE PLAY

When your guard and tackle candidates line up on the opening day of spring practice, size them up carefully. Have them perform wind sprints daily, in order that you may know just who are the fastest men on the squad. These sprints consist of fifty-yard dashes at top speed. The general rule is that the tackles should be the biggest men on the team. However, if you can find a big man who is exceptionally fast at starting and pulling out of the line, you may well have yourself an All-American guard in the making. Our 1948 captain, Bill Fischer, came to Notre Dame as a tackle, and in view of his 235 pounds that was the logical spot for him. Frequently in practice we would notice Bill as one of the first men to move in the line. We gave him a try at left guard, a position that calls for a lot of pulling in our offense, and before the season was three weeks old he was a candidate for All-American honors at the guard post. Bill excels at downfield blocking, and to have him playing offensive tackle would be wasting considerable talent. If you have such a man as Fischer, and I certainly hope that many coaches will have, it might be a good move to use him as a guard offensively and a tackle defensively. This move will give the needed weight at the tackle spot plus the speed at the guard position. Such a switch will not only give added strength to the line but will help to confuse the opponents.

15

Center Play

THE CENTER is without a doubt one of the most valuable men in the whole offensive set-up of the "T" formation. If you do not have a good center who is quick and fast, then by all means start looking for one. Sometimes you may find a very good fullback who is just a little slow. He may be just the man you are looking for. We used Marty Wendell at center one year before moving him again to guard, and he performed admirably at the pivot post. We have had some exceptionally good "T" centers at Notre Dame, and we like to think the main reason they turned out so well is that they were willing to pay the price for success. They would work tirelessly trying to draw blood from the quarterback's hands. Such names as Wally Ziemba, Herb Coleman, Frank Syzmanski, George Strohmeyer, and Bill Walsh will always be referred to when people are speaking of good "T" formation centers—and they were good because they wanted to be good.

Until your center and quarterback function properly together you are not going to have much success with this formation. They are the heart and soul of the system, and in some instances you will find it takes hours to bring them to a point where they can operate as one. When the automatic exchange becomes as natural as their breathing, then you have the correct combination. Advise your center to study the quarterback's personality, in order that he may surmise how the signal caller is likely to react under certain circumstances.

STANCE

Our center places himself over the ball with his feet spread just as wide as possible; yet we want him to stand in a position where he can still move forward at the moment the ball is snapped. One reason for asking our center to be at his maximum width is that it causes the defense to expand. If all the linemen down the way spread out in such a manner, it causes wider holes along the center of the defensive line. When the holes are fairly wide, a quick-opener can be run before the enemy has time to move over and close them up. The center's toes should be pointing straight ahead at all times, and he should have his left foot flat on the ground. (Once again we are assuming that all the centers are right-handed; the instructions would be just the opposite in the case of a left-handed pivot man.) As to the right foot, the center has his heel lifted about two inches, and all of the weight coming directly on the ball of his foot. Our centers line up with the weight distributed in the above manner in order to allow themselves to go forward and make contact with the enemy as quickly as possible.

HEAD POSITION

Next we ask our center to overexaggerate his position over the ball. This is especially true of his head position. We have him hold his head up in such a manner as to make his neck muscles very sore. Just ask him to force himself to hold his head back a little longer each day, until this becomes natural. We have noticed, as many have, I am sure, that most centers in the "T" formation have their heads up only slightly. That is correct. But if the head is up only slightly

and they start charging forward, they will find after they
have made contact and have taken a few steps that they are
hitting too low, and that their head is going down. By
means of this unusual exaggeration—and we work on it every
day—the center soon becomes 100 percent a blocker, and he
knows what is going on all of the time he is scuffling with the
opponent. Try it yourself sometime and you will notice
how sore your neck muscles become at first. We have known
many of our centers who have had to increase the size of their
collars one whole inch during the course of a football season.
If the boy is in the position we have just described, he sees
better, and when he goes for the enemy it is natural that he
block a little higher, thus remaining with his opponent for a
few more seconds and a few extra steps.

The right foot of the center is dropped back slightly, which
puts it in a position to cause the quarterback trouble if he
is planning on crossing over when he receives the ball. In
view of this, we have our centers start to pull their right
foot forward as they begin to snap the ball back. Therefore,
we always have our centers stepping off with their right foot
as they start to make the offensive maneuver. Impress upon
your centers how important it is that they get that right foot
out of the way before the quarterback goes into his spinning
processes. (Following page 132 is a photo of center Walt
Grothaus, illustrating the correct offensive stance for his position.)

GRASPING THE BALL

Next we stress the importance of the center exerting
plenty of weight on the football. He should put as much
pressure as he possibly can on the ball, with both hands grasping it. The left hand should be back toward the rear tip
of the ball, and we like to have the right hand away out in

front. We have discovered that our center can do a much better job of driving the ball into the quarterback's hands swiftly and effectively if he will have his right hand placed up on the top of the ball rather than underneath it. The latter method seems to be the common tendency, but experience has taught us that the former will produce better results. This permits the center to have better control of the ball as he is snapping it back to the signal caller.

Our right-handed centers turn the ball just about one-half an inch to the left, and tilt it as much as they can—that is, just as much as the officials will permit. We realize that the ball cannot be tilted away up in the air, but it can be given just a slight tilt, and if we have this type of angle on the ball, we will always find that the right hand is up, not under. If the center has his hand under the ball, he has a natural tendency to lift the ball when moving it back. On the other hand, if he has his right hand on top, he will find that he can drive the ball back very rapidly and that it will hit into the quarterback's hands exactly as we desire. If these simple rules are carried out, the quarterback will be ready to go into his spin as soon as he receives the ball from the center. To recapitulate, we have the left hand back, the right hand on top, the left foot flat, and the right heel raised, as we begin to move the ball.

THE SNAPBACK

A very natural fault that we find in all beginning "T" formation centers is that they have a tendency to lift the ball and then start after their opponent. That is a little too late to start doing business. We want—in fact, we insist upon it—our centers to go forward as they start to drive the ball back. This can be worked into one very smooth maneuver if the men will only put in the required amount of time to perfect it. It is almost like a track man's gestures. That is, as his hand is going back, his foot is kicking forward. This gives the man the proper balance and timing to carry out his individual assignment. Drill your centers on this until you notice them taking pride in the easy manner in which they incorporate these two important steps into one smooth stride. The center, if he is going to be 100 percent a blocker, must do these two things at exactly the same time. Very often you will find that this one maneuver is the difference between a yard and one-half or no gain at all.

We believe that our center should be the best offensive lineman we have, and we never hesitate to pass this information along to our candidates for this position. We feel that it is a very good thing, from a psychological standpoint, to inform our center that he should be the finest and most effective blocker in our line. Our reason for believing this is because this man knows better than anyone else in the entire stadium when the ball is going to be snapped, for the simple reason that he is the one doing the snapping. We find that if we impress continually upon individual players the importance of their position to the success of the team as a unit, they work harder at their daily tasks. As the center drives the ball back, he should be on his opponent. If it is a small yardage situation and we are trying to force our way through the center of the line, we find that the center usually has the big jump on the man across the line, and we have a yard before the linebackers can move up.

BLOCKING BY THE CENTER

When the center does not have a man playing opposite him, we like to have him take part in our downfield blocking activities. Speed is one asset that we always like to find in a center. We look for speed because we do not ask him to sprint out and veer in the general direction of the ball carrier, as we do our other linemen on such a play. Rather, we have

the center take two steps behind the line of scrimmage as soon as the ball leaves his hands. Once behind the enemy wall he should turn on a ninety-degree angle and head toward the spot where the ball carrier will be coming through. From then on he should act as a part of the interference. He should be just about as fast as our fullback, and should experience no difficulty in clearing the field for his teammate. Usually the center more closely resembles a back than anyone that we find in the line. That is why many coaches convert their fullbacks into centers.

BLOCKING IN THE LINE OF SCRIMMAGE

When the center is blocking in the line of scrimmage he should always take short digging steps. The legs should never be completely extended. He should always have a little flex left in the knees. When the ball is snapped he should move like a cat toward his target. His eyes must be wide open and he must keep them on the target until the block is completed. Do not allow him to watch the opponent's head, or he may be faked right out of the play. We ask our men to keep their eyes on the enemy's midsection, which is a spot that the man cannot fake in and out of position. The body in motion naturally follows the position of the head; therefore, the head must be up in order to react swiftly to the opponent's change of position.

An important rule that we always put across to our centers on offense is that they must get their head between the defender and the ball carrier when they are making their block. That is, if the ball carrier is running to the center's right he should block with his left shoulder. If you will just analyze such a situation for a few seconds, you will realize how imprudent it is for a lineman to block any other way. Yet it is done all too often on Saturday afternoons.

Our method not only makes it easier for the center to block the man out of the play, but it also permits him to use split vision to inform him when he can release his block and head into the front lines.

A man who is standing erect may present a higher target than one who is in a lineman's defensive stance. We tell our boys that they never should be afraid of blocking too high. It is true that a man can block too high, but the natural tendency is to block too low, and we have never run into any difficulty as a result of our linemen blocking too high. As soon as the ball leaves his hand the center should strive diligently to assume a position whereby the potential tackler will have to come directly through him if he plans on making the tackle. Such a position will definitely restrict the area in which the defender can maneuver. The center should always attack the defender and not the position. However, the center does have the distinct advantage of knowing just where the ball carrier will be going, and thus he does not have to make any extensive effort to chase a defender who is moving away from the hole. In this regard, we have our centers approach the defender directly, and if the latter is moving away, we do not want our center to throw his body wildly into space just for the sake of making an effort. We want him to block hard on his target, but not until his target is ready to be blocked. His short digging steps should bring him almost upon the enemy before he makes his contact. If the center gets in close before applying the pressure, then he will have lots of time to do plenty of scuffling with his opponent.

DOWNFIELD BLOCKING

When the center is called upon to participate in the downfield blocking, he must bear in mind always that he will be

attacking a desperate, fighting man. The enemy he is called upon to remove from the scene may be the opponent's last hope between victory and defeat, and you can rest assured that he will not make things pleasant for your center. Every block that is executed while running at full speed must have body control and aggressiveness. We find that, as a rule, the downfield blockers always want to leave their feet too soon. One thing we ask them to do when they are just about to block the defensive back is to take one more step after they feel that they are ready to make contact. This extra step brings them close enough really to halt the opponent when they apply pressure to him. If the center is the only downfield blocker with the ball carrier, he should attempt to block the man and keep his feet. This should never be done at the expense of making a poor block, however. In case there is another teammate ready to escort the ball carrier, we like to see our center leave his feet and make a good body block on the defender. When such a solid block is made on one occasion, I believe you will notice that the same defender is a little reluctant to crash right through the next time a similar situation arises.

TYPES OF BLOCKS

Blocking for centers comes under three general classifications. First, we have the shoulder block; second, the cross body block; and third, the reverse body block. In "T" formation line play the shoulder block is by far the most common. This is what we always call for on our quick-opening plays, when all we ask of the center is that he keep his opponent occupied long enough for the halfback to go through the hole. Blocking in this manner can be made easy if the centers will spend some of their spare time thinking of little tricks to force the enemy into an advantageous blocking angle. The simplest, and yet the most effective of all such tricks, is the head fake. We have our assistant coaches drill the boys on this continually when they are working out in groups. If our man just moves his head in the appropriate direction, it will cause the man across the line to shift his weight momentarily, thus leaving him vulnerable to a good, solid shoulder block. Such little "extras" as the head fake are the coach's responsibility. The majority of boys who come out for football have the general idea of how it is played, and many have the physical requirements to help make them outstanding players. If the coach will take time to teach all of his lads the little tricks that he has picked up during his years of experience, he will notice that the good men are becoming great.

The cross body block can be used frequently by the center when he is called upon to block one of the men backing up the line. For the best results the center should sprint a short distance beyond the man and then cut back on him. This will cause the opponent to be heading up into the line, and the center can throw his entire body at the front side of the enemy. Such a block should be used only when the center feels that a shoulder block definitely would prove ineffective.

When a shoulder block has been applied and the man is beginning to slip away, in toward the scene of activities, it is the correct time for the center to employ the reverse body block. Imagine that the center has his right shoulder buried in the opponent's midsection, and is taking his short digging steps in an attempt to drive the opponent out toward the right sideline. He then begins to feel that the opponent is easing away from him and may get into the offensive backfield in time to cause trouble. It is at this time that the center should spring into action. He should take one rather large step forward with his right foot, and as it hits the ground, he must pivot around to his left—that is, away from the enemy—and then throw his entire body at the opponent.

The pivot takes him around 180 degrees from the position he was in when his right foot hit the gridiron. This is known as the reverse body block, and it has proved exceptionally useful to our centers when they want to make certain that a hole remains open long enough for the ball carrier to make his way through.

The pass block is another type that we teach separately. We like to have our center use varied tactics on passes in order that he will not give away the play. The most common pass block is to have the man come up tall and block with his entire body in an upright position. In this manner he can give a little ground to the opponent but can still obstruct his view of the passer. Another time we might have our center jump across the line with a quick shoulder block before coming up straight to go into his tall body block. We set forth these two patterns for our men on pass plays, but then we tell them that our main concern is that the passer have enough time to get rid of the ball. If they truthfully feel that they can employ some method which will allow them to do a better job of keeping the passer untouched, then we advise them to do so. We say this in regard to pass protection because it is one phase of offensive football where you do not have a set procedure. There is no definite hole, and many times the passer has to move around in the backfield to locate his target. Thus, we give our centers a little bit of free rein as to how they should block the enemy.

BLOCKING ERRORS

Whenever our blocking fails, we have found that it usually is due to one of the following mistakes. These rules are not invariable, but you will find that you can very seldom lay the blame for a poor block on a reason that is not listed here.

First is tipping-off of the assignment. Many centers are

so anxious to get out to make their block that they begin to look the man over before they have released the ball.

Second, we find that too many men lose their feet after the initial contact has been made. This is due to the fact that they are taking too large a step. The short digging steps will allow them to keep their footing under almost every kind of scuffling conditions.

Third, we have noticed that many men lose their aggressive spirit as soon as they make the contact. If anything, the blocker should work harder after he meets the man than he did while coming toward him. An aggressive blocker is always a dangerous man, since he can often put across the important drive as the enemy takes a split second to relax.

The fourth fault is that the blocker starts to move too slowly. As we said before, the center should be the first man in the stadium to start producing. As soon as he feels the pigskin hit the quarterback's hands he should be on his way across the line.

Fifth is a fault that is inexcusable—that is, uncertainty of assignment. We spend a great deal of our time during our noon meetings going over the individual assignments of each and every player. We welcome questions at these meetings, and when we do not get them, we just naturally assume that the boys know what their duties are on every play in our attack.

Sixth, and last, is a trait that we will not tolerate on our squad, and that is loafing. We would like to take time to teach the boy how this habit can follow him all through life, but since we have so little time for anything other than the bare fundamentals, we just put him back on the bench. If he has sufficient character and spirit, he will be back on the starting lineup. If not, we are not interested in having him represent our Alma Mater on the football field.

We will bring this chapter to a close with the message that

we give to all of our players when we start them in as blockers. We tell them first that they must master the technique of blocking. Next, they must know exactly what is to be accomplished, and lastly, they must make a determined and aggressive effort to accomplish it.

16

Punt and Kickoff Returns

RETURNING KICKS has developed into a major part of the offensive football set-up today. The free substitution rule, which permits us to have our scatbacks in the lineup at the time we expect the enemy to kick, has caused football coaches to spend much of their time planning a definite method of returning punts and kickoffs. By assigning every member of our team a certain task on kicks, we have set up an offense which, if each man carries out his assignment, will result in a touchdown. We work on the idea that with eleven men on each team the offense should be able to shake the receiver loose before the opposition gets into position.

PUNT RETURNS

First we will discuss the assignments on a punt return, as we have diagrammed it on page 189. The defense we have set up when preparing to punt is one that we use quite often; that is, the balanced line with the right end spread wide. We frequently spread the end on the wide side of the field in order to force the ball carrier to cut back toward the center of the gridiron. Our backfield lines up with the two halfbacks in approximately the same position as for all "T" plays. The fullback is about three yards behind the right halfback, and concentrates on the opposing left end. The quarterback, or whoever is doing your kicking, should assume his position approximately ten yards behind the center.

Hereafter we shall assume that we are the team that is going to receive the punt. Our *left end* crashes fast in an

attempt to block the punt.   After making an all-out attempt to block the kick he should veer sharply to his right
and cut back for the purpose of joining his teammates in clearing a path for the man who catches the ball.   In so far as is
practical, we have our quarterback inform all of the men
prior to a punt as to on which side of the field our ball car-

Punt return to the right:

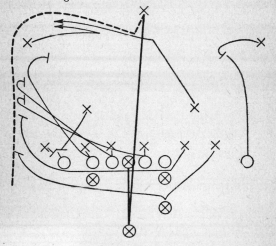

Punt return to the left:

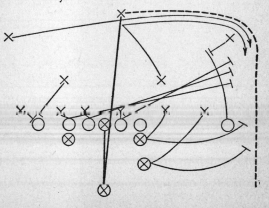

rier will run.   Once this is settled, we ask the receivers to follow that procedure unless it is absolutely impossible to do so.

Our *left tackle* should come up and in fast, but not too
far.   As soon as he sees that the punt is away he too should
veer off to his right and hustle back to join the fracas.   Our
left guard should make one good, solid head fake at the man
on his head before pulling back to join the interference.   The
right guard should make the same type of head fake before
cutting back to get into position.   We ask our *right tackle*
to take one step in with his left foot toward the opposing
tackle before pulling back to act as a blocker.   Before going
any further with the assignments we want to point out how
we like to have our men form when they gather on the right-
hand sideline.   We ask our *right tackle* to get as near to the
ball carrier as possible and make it a point to take care of the
first enemy who appears in the path.   The *right guard* should
come up on the outside of the tackle, with the *left guard*
swinging even wider.   As the *left tackle* and *left end* come
around from the enemy secondary they should scan the field
and pick out the spot where they believe they can do the most
good for their ball-carrying teammate.   Instruct them to
think always in terms of what one man can do to spoil the
return.   If they have this in mind, they will work that much
harder to see that every member of the opposition is oblit-
erated from the path of the ball carrier.

The *right end* double teams with our *center* to block the
offensive *left end*.   This is when we are in a normal six-man
line, with the center backing up the line on the right side.
These two men must work hard on the enemy end since he
is in a position to get downfield before our linemen have an
opportunity to pull back and block.   If this man is stopped
at the line of scrimmage, your ball carrier should have a successful return trip.   The *fullback,* who is backing up the
line on the left-hand side, pivots and runs back to lead the
interference.   As soon as he sees it is going to be a kick he

should turn, and when he hears the thud he should start moving toward his teammate. The *right halfback* holds his position until he sees where the kick is going and then sprints over to act as a blocker. Many teams will punt away from the safety man, thus giving the halfbacks an opportunity to return the kick. Our *left halfback* has a very important job; that is, to block the offensive right end as he comes down the field. The enemy wingman will have picked up speed and momentum and will be a tough man with whom to do business. If the halfback will make the end swing around him so that he can throw a long body block on this man, the latter should be too late to cause any trouble.

Should the kick go to either of the halfbacks, the *safety* man should sprint up quickly and strive to remove the first potential tackler from the path. In these diagrams we have assumed that the quarterback is the safety man, although many teams, including Notre Dame on various occasions, have one of their halfbacks in that position when a kick is in the offing. We have outlined a punt return to both the right and left sides of the field, and the only difference is that the corresponding man on the opposite side of the line carries out the explained assignments. We would like to suggest that coaches keep their kicking plans simple, for with so much commotion going on, complications make it difficult for the players to locate their positions in an open field. It is our belief that the two methods diagrammed will fill the bill for all punt returns. Another suggestion is that coaches look deep into their material for a good man to return kicks. Give all of the small men a try at this task. Frequently you will find that a boy who is too small for any other use will be your most valuable man for bringing back a punt. These men have the knack of picking their way through an open field and ending up in the end zone. For three years the smallest member of our squad was our best man on returning kicks.

KICKOFF RETURNS

The kickoff return that we have outlined here is one of our favorite plays, since it did more to relieve the pressure on the writer than any play we have ever used. It was the opening play of our game with Army in 1947, when the tension was at its peak. The West Pointers kicked a beautiful end-over-end ball, which was picked up by Terry Brennan on our three-yard line. The interference formed exactly as it always had in our dreams, and before the game was eighteen seconds old we were leading one of America's greatest teams by six points. Some excellent blocks were thrown on the run by our center, Bill Walsh, our ends Jim Martin and Leon Hart, and our defensive ace, Russell Ashbaugh.

On page 193 we have diagrammed a field from the forty-yard line, where the kicker lines up. With free substitution most teams have their best tacklers in at this time, so we will not designate the opponents by position. Our front line, which consists of the five middle linemen, assumes its position on the fifty-yard line, ready for action. The two ends get into position on the thirty-yard line and directly behind our tackles. The number one defensive back lines up on the twenty yard line facing the kicker. Two of the running backs station themselves on the ten-yard line, fairly close to the sidelines, while the scatback locates on the five-yard line in the center of the field. With this plan we have every available section of the playing field covered.

We will assume that the kick is a good one that comes down to the *left halfback* on about the eleven-yard line. After "looking" the ball into his hands, he starts his trek up the gridiron. We ask our ball carriers to run directly toward the back who is stationed at the twenty in the middle of the field. This maneuver centralizes the play and draws the first tackler right into an able blocker. After reaching this point the ball carrier should "belly" slightly and head for the opposite

sideline. The reason for the sweep is to allow the linemen to
get back in time to apply their blocks. We do not assign
anyone to the men coming up on the opposite side of the field,
but we do have a few of our linemen get into positions that
would discourage such men from cutting across.

We have numbered the potentially dangerous opponents
in order that their actions may be followed easily. Our *right
end* takes the number two enemy as he comes straight up the
field. The task here is to see that the man is driven in toward
the center of the field, thus allowing our back to sweep wide.
The *right tackle* pivots toward the outside and sprints up to
throw a long body block on the number three man. These
men should be running almost parallel to each other, and as

Kickoff return:

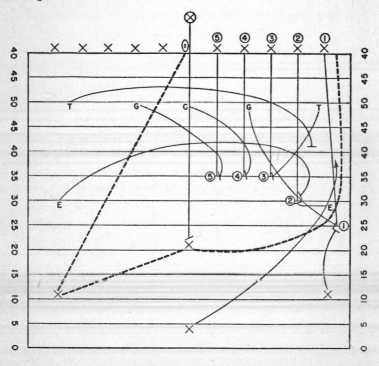

the opponent cuts in, he should be blocked fiercely. We have our fast-stepping *right guard* pivot in and dash back to double team with the *right halfback* on the number one member of the opposition. This is an important assignment because we desire to have this man driven out toward the sideline so that the man with the ball can cut inside of him. Teamwork will insure good results on this play. The *center* pivots to his right and swings wide to circumvent the number four man. His block will be similar to that thrown by the tackle and should be fairly easy to accomplish. The *left guard* draws a like assignment in that he pivots to his right and sweeps around the number five opponent, blocking him toward the center of the field.

Our *left tackle* and *left end* do not draw specific assignments. We ask them to sprint over into the front lines and block back on any men who are sifting over or who have recovered from the initial blocks placed on them. Their task is very important, since it usually is the man you do not expect to do so who upsets the applecart. Our *defensive back* who was located on the twenty-yard line has the all-important duty of blocking the man who kicked off. This is why we have the back run toward this man; the kicker is the first man downfield and invariably the most dangerous. We ask our man to apply a long body block on him and strive diligently to see that he is not the man who stops the ball carrier. As mentioned, the *right halfback* double teams with the guard on the number one man, while the safety man leads the interference as the *left halfback* heads goalward.

This kickoff plan is one that depends heavily on hustle and team spirit. We designate the man who is playing in the defensive back spot to call out whether the return is to be run to the right or to the left after he sees who is going to get the ball. His call informs our linemen which way they are to come back. If the call is to the left, the men just change assignments with their teammate on the opposite side of the line. Good, sharp blocking will clear the path quickly; it can be attained because the opponents are coming at full speed, and when they are hit, they will go down.

This is the type of play to which coaches should devote time on the day before a game, in dummy maneuvers. No one will get hurt, and it will sharpen up the lads as to how they may score six easy points. An abundance of determination and drive on the part of eleven men will make this play one of the most successful in the book.

Our toughest game in many years came at the conclusion of the 1948 season, when Southern California was leading our unbeaten Irish, 14 to 7, with less than two minutes remaining in the game. It was at this time that Southern California kicked off to 155-pound Billy Gay, who received the ball on our own five-yard line. From that spot he followed the path taken by the ball carrier in the diagram, and traveled eighty-six yards before being stopped. The combination of excellent running and outstanding blocking put us into scoring position, and Emil Sitko scored on a simple "43." At no time in my coaching career have I ever been as proud of my team as I was when they refused to accept defeat in this game. In effect, that team possessed the *burning desire to win* to the highest possible degree.

17

Defensive Football

O UR COACHING STAFF is unanimous in the opinion
that the most fundamental phase in football is tackling.
We tell our squad members that they *cannot win without the
ball,* and they will never gain possession of the pigskin if they
do not stop the opponent from advancing it. The best way
to put a halt to the enemy action is by means of good solid
tackles.

Oftentimes you hear it said in the sports world that "The
best defense is a good offense." Yet it is my most firm conviction that in football the reverse is actually true—and that
is, "The best offense is a good defense." The greatest scoring
power in the world cannot register six points unless they have
the ball in their possession, and the only way to keep the
pigskin continually is to tackle the opponent as if you really
mean business.

TACKLING

BASIC RULES FOR TACKLING

We have laid down some basic rules for tackling that we
sincerely believe must be adhered to absolutely by each and
every player in order to have a successful team in this era of
speed and deception. First and foremost is that which our
players hear about continually from the coaching staff, and
that is, they must possess a burning desire to tackle the man
with the ball. We do not feel that we can talk too much

about this desire because without it you will have just another football team, whereas with it you can have a great team. A tackler should not just bump into the ball carrier and hope to knock him down. He must encircle him with both arms, bring him all the way to the ground, and not release his grasp until the whistle stops the play. If the ball carrier is aggressive, the tackler must be more aggressive. The majority of the time you will find that the potential tackler will outweigh the ball carrier, and he should use this advantage to its fullest extent.

Defensive men must look the situation over thoroughly and visualize in their own mind what play they would call if they were the opposing quarterback. What would be the most logical play to run? If it is second and thirteen, it is safe to assume that the opponent may employ a pass play. When they have the general idea firmly set in their mind, then they will be ready to react as soon as the ball is snapped. Defenders should always tense themselves to react as appropriate for the way they think the play is going, but they should hold a little in reserve in case the opposing signal caller crosses them up.

A good tackler will never reach for the ball carrier. He will run directly at him. A favorite phrase that we always give to our tacklers is, "Sprint to him—then sprint through him." By this we mean, do not stop before you get to the man and then attempt to reach out and grab him. A tackler should keep charging until his shoulder is buried deep in the man's midsection; then he must keep churning his legs into the ground until the man goes all the way to the turf. Make sure that the shoulder is there and not the head, since this is a very easy way to obtain a serious head injury.

If your head is up, then you will be up! If your head goes down, you will go down! It is common knowledge that a man who has his head down may as well be blind. Always be on the alert; know what is going on every minute of the game.   This cannot possibly be achieved if your head is down.

We ask our tackler to follow the man all the way to the turf.   As soon as he grasps the ball carrier he should start immediately to take short choppy steps; he should keep pumping his legs until the ball carrier has gone all the way down to the ground or until the whistle has *definitely* stopped the play.   This is exceptionally important, because as a general rule ball carriers are lighter than the potential tackler, which gives the man with the ball an opportunity to slip away if the defensive player does not stick with him until he is positively grounded.

Tacklers must keep high and know how the play is progressing.   Many backs like to hurdle the defensive man.   Although this is a dangerous practice, it sometimes works for all-important yardage.   The so-called "shoestring tackle" is no longer recognized as the perfect method of stopping a runner.   Although this type of tackle is highly effective when performed correctly, the chances of missing the man are altogether too great to take the unnecessary risk.

We want our men to interlock their hands at every possible opportunity when tackling.   They are not able to do this very often, but it is the perfect method, and we ask our men to strive for perfection in every move they make.   Every time they make a tackle they should strive diligently to achieve this objective, and they should come as close to encircling the man as they possibly can.

Eyes must be open at all times.   Linebackers should always be on the alert for a quick movement by the ball carrier intended to throw them out of position.   If there is ever a doubt in the mind as to whether the ball carrier intends to lateral or not, make certain the defender is on the outside of the play.   By this we mean, if it looks like a lateral to the outside man, the defender must go after the latter and force the ball carrier in toward his teammates.   In this manner, if there is a lateral, then he will get the correct man, and if not, the ball carrier will be driven into a section of the field where there are many potential tacklers.

Tactics should be varied to keep the opponent guessing. Have the men crash one time, drift the next, and combine these methods when defending the goal. If the man across the line is worried about how you plan to come in, then he will not be able to do his job 100 percent.

TACKLING BY LINEBACKERS

Linebackers should always say to themselves, "It's going to be a pass," until they definitely know otherwise. All of the above information given to the linemen on tackling applies to them also, but the men behind the line should be just a little more cautious before they drive in to make the tackle. They should analyze the situation quickly and carefully before making a move that might throw them out of position. Whenever a ball carrier is sweeping wide, they should not overrun him. We ask them to move like cats, with the body ready to spring in either direction when the runner makes his bid to come up to the line of scrimmage. A common fault of linebackers on end sweeps is to dash over to the sidelines, and a good runner can make a sharp cutback and pick up many valuable yards before the rest of the defense can catch up with him. Ask your linebackers to play basketball during the off season. This will keep their footwork in shape and make them react faster in all directions. It does not have to be varsity basketball, just so long as they get out on the court and are scrambling for the ball.

HELPFUL DEFENSIVE TACTICS

All linemen should capture one yard on the offensive team. As soon as the ball is snapped they should gain one step across the line by means of all the various methods in use today. Have them try the shoulder drop one time, bringing their elbows high on the next, and, if they are big enough, just forcing their way over now and then. They must protect their own zone first. If the ball carrier starts off in another direction, the defender must make absolutely certain that there is no possibility of his cutting back into the zone before he leaves it to chase him.

FOLLOW THE BALL

Linebackers should move toward the ball, always keeping the same distance away from their teammates as they were in the line of scrimmage. As they break through the line, they must veer off together in pursuit of the ball carrier, and they thus will look like an organized unit for the full sixty minutes every Saturday afternoon.

We tell our linemen never to look through the line at "T" formation backs. This can be the undoing of even the greatest linemen. These nifty little backs have many tricks that they employ to deceive the opposing linemen as to where they plan to run. Some make feet maneuvers, others head fakes, while some look continually at one spot in the line and then run in just the opposite direction. Linemen must always look straight ahead, watching the ball with split vision.

"Stay as low as you can as long as you can." This is one of the cardinal rules for linemen, both on offense and defense. We want our linemen to do this so that they will not be knocked down very easily. A man who is moving around in an upright position always makes a much better target than does one who is in a semi-crouch. They should keep driving in this position until it is absolutely necessary to come into an upright stance.

EVERY MAN RESPONSIBLE

If every member of the team will feel that it is his sole responsibility to bring down the ball carrier, I firmly believe
that you will not see very many of your opponents scurrying
into the end zone. No man should ever stop chasing the
runner until the whistle has stopped the play. We often recall a very unfortunate incident in this regard, which occurred during our game with the Great Lakes Naval Training Station in 1943. The "Bluejackets" fullback had broken
through the left side of our line, but was apparently hemmed
in by our linebackers on that side of the field. Assuming
this to be the case, our remaining men stopped to watch the
proceedings. The Great Lakes man did not want to be tackled and he broke loose. Before our other men could get over
to him it was too late. We lost that ball game, 19 to 13. It
was our only defeat during the 1943 season.

Instruct your tacklers to be "ball hawks." We want them
to know where the ball is for every minute of the game and
to get as close to it as they possibly can. When tackling a
man, they should look to see where the pigskin is. Frequently
when a player is tackled hard he will momentarily lose his
grasp on the ball. A wide-awake tackler might be able to
take the ball into his possession. During our game with
Southern California in 1947 we had a third string man named
Al Zmijewski playing right tackle. When the ball was
snapped, Al broke through the line as the Trojans were starting to run a play similar to our "29H." The ball was hardly
out of the quarterback's hands when Al intercepted it and ran
fifty-nine yards to a touchdown.

Linemen should take every inch of space that is rightfully
theirs when they line up. They should get as near to the ball
as they possibly can without being offside. Even a fraction

of an inch may give the needed jump on the opposing linemen.

Each player on defense should use his head at all times. When the men see an opponent make a certain move, they should try to figure out why he made such a move, and act accordingly. The type of block the opposing linemen attempt to use often gives away their offensive plan. When a man tries to block high, they can assume that a pass is probably in the making. If such is the case, and the lineman is in a spot to bottle up the end for a few seconds, he should do so. This will cut down the number of eligible pass receivers and make things easier for the backfield men. A defender should never allow a runner to get outside of him. It is better to let him run inside than to make a desperation tackle as he is sweeping wide. Tacklers should always operate with the thought in mind that their teammates are in a position to come up fast if they miss the man, so make him cut in a direction that will allow them to be of assistance. This rule applies especially to ends, but frequently the corner linebackers find themselves in a similar position.

During practice we ask our corner linebackers to keep their eyes on their own zone. That is their number one problem. They must watch the men closely who operate in that area. Many times the overanxious linemen will give a tip-off that will help immeasurably. As a general rule, we like to have our corner linebackers keep their eyes on the tackle and end of the offensive unit. By making them directly responsible for this certain zone, we find that we achieve better results. We do not want the linebackers to watch the backs any more than we want our linemen to commit this error. The middle backer-up has the two guards and the center under his surveillance. If the three backers-up will watch the movements of the seven men in the line, they will be able to obtain a very good idea of what kind of play is about to unfold. Watch constantly for tip-offs, especially when the going is tough; the opponents may be overanxious to get into action.

We like to have our backfield men call out to their teammates as soon as they have definitely sensed what type of play
is being run. These backfield men must be even more cautious than the linebackers, since they are the last hope of stopping the ball carrier.

DEFENSIVE STANCE

In regard to the stance of the linemen, we have found that
the conventional three point stance brings the best results.
This method, with one foot behind the other, gives the lineman that leverage which is needed for him to charge across
the line and gain the upper hand on his opponent. The offense has the big advantage of knowing when the ball is going
to be snapped, and to overcome it, the defense must react in-
stantly, or just as rapidly as they possibly can.

We allow our ends to use their own judgment on what type
of stance they employ. We do ask that they vary their tactics, but it is up to the individual as to how he lines up.

OUTSTANDING DEFENSIVE MANEUVERS

There are a few incidents which occurred during some of
our Notre Dame games that we like to point out as concrete
examples of excellent defensive play. Many people still talk
about the manner in which Johnny Lujack stopped Doc Blanchard in the open field during our o to o game with Army
in 1946. Blanchard had cut off left tackle and was well on
his way toward breaking that tie score. Johnny came up fast
from his safety position and forced Blanchard in toward the
sideline, until it was necessary for the runner to do one of
three things. He could have stepped out of bounds, but
that was not a habit of his. Or he could have cut back to-

ward the middle of the field. The third alternative was to attempt to bull his way past our safety man, as he had done successfully so many times in the past against other opponents. He tried the third method, but Lujack possessed just a little too much of that burning desire to stop him. Johnny hit him at the knees, circled him with both arms, and brought that terrific fullback to the ground. John Lujack has performed so admirably for Notre Dame on the football field that it would be extremely difficult to point out any one maneuver as being his finest, but I can say for certain that the one just described did more to prevent the head coach from having a heart attack than any other I can recall.

We had a young man at Notre Dame whose name is Russell Ashbaugh. He loved to play defensive football, and derived as much enjoyment from making a good solid tackle as any other back would get out of scoring six points. On the opening play of the second half in our game with Pittsburgh in 1947 the Pitt left halfback received the kickoff and was headed for pay territory. As he came down the left sideline, he picked up two blockers before he came to Ashbaugh, who was playing the safety position at that time. Russ analyzed the situation before moving in. As soon as he was close enough for contact he made a strong head fake in one direction and immediately dove between the two blockers from another angle. He stopped the ball carrier and Pitt's chances to score six points.

One of the greatest examples of defensive teamwork was displayed by Terry Brennan and John Lujack in our game with Iowa in the 1947 season. Iowa came out in the second half using the old Notre Dame box formation. Emlen Tunnell, their speedy halfback, started to sweep his own right end. As he was going wide, he noticed that our linebackers were overrunning him, so he cut back toward the center of the field. By the time he had reached the other sideline he had picked up two blockers and was on his way to glory.   At this point Lujack came up fast and started to parry with the blockers.   He would jump in and bump them and then jump back.   He kept doing this until Brennan was able to get past the occupied blockers and make the touchdown-saving tackle. Plays such as the ones we have just described make a coach feel that he has been able to instill something in his players besides the overwhelming desire to score touchdowns.

We have found, without fail, that the men who are good tacklers are always fine young American gentlemen.   It takes a tremendous amount of character to become a good tackler. I say this because I know that it requires much sacrifice and hard work—and there is very little glory to be derived from making a tackle.   About all a player gets out of tackling a man is an abundance of personal satisfaction, and for a good American youth that is all that is needed.

Remind your players that if they will keep their eyes open, their heads up, and possess that burning desire to stop the ball carrier, there will be very few men who will ever get behind them.

18

Pass Defense

THE MODERN TREND in football has made pass defense one of the most important phases of the game. Almost every top team of the past few years was great because they had exceptionally fine passers. Such men as John Lujack, Frank Tripucka, Bob Chappuis, Charley Conerly, Bobby Layne, Perry Moss, Bob DeMoss, Al DeMarco, Johnny Rauch, and a great many others have forced coaches to spend much of their time devising a defense that would at least slow down the attempts of these great passers.

REQUISITES FOR PASS DEFENSE

We teach pass defense in a set pattern to which we ask each member of our team to adhere, because in our heart we believe that it is positively the best defense we are capable of establishing. Without any question the number one requisite of a pass defender is that he must have the burning desire to prevent the opponent from completing a forward pass. Each year when we ask our lads to call out the various requirements we always get a perfect response on this first point.

Aggressiveness is the second point, and we tell our boys that when the football is in the air it belongs to the first person who gets his hands on it. It is a free ball, and if the defender will get over to it in time, he can battle for the ball without coming close to interfering with the receiver.

All defensive backs must know what the situation is at all times. Naturally, if they are cognizant of the down and the yardage situation, they can figure out just about what the enemy will have to call.

BACKS AND LINEBACKERS ON PASS DEFENSE

COVERING THE RECEIVER

The number one "don't" for a pass defender is never to let a man get behind him. This mistake has been the cause of more football coaches going gray-headed than any other item in the book. Insist that the defenders stick with the man as he comes down into their zone. If he cuts out of the zone, they should not go with him unless the ball is in the air. A favorite trick of a good passing team is to send two men into a zone, and let the first man draw the defender out of the area.

Linebackers should slow up the ends, by making them go around or else block on the backer-up. When the backer-up puts himself in a fairly good spot to be blocked and the end veers away, it is time for the linebacker to notify his teammates that a pass is in the offing.

When the defender is running downfield with the potential receiver he should turn his entire body toward the goal line he is defending while keeping his head turned fixedly toward the passer. He should watch the receiver with split vision, but must not let the passer out of his sight until the ball is in the air. A good passer will try very hard to fake the defender out of position by turning and faking a pass out toward the flat. A top flight pass defender will never move away from his man until he sees the ball in the air.

The defender must keep his eyes on the midsection of the receiver as the latter is coming down the field. All good pass receivers like to fake the defender out by moving their head or by a fast cross-over movement with their legs. The defender should never approach nearer than to within three yards of the receiver. If he is any closer, the defender is much too vulnerable to a fake. He should stick with his man and play his zone until the ball is in the air.

FLAT PASSES

On flat passes the halfbacks should not come up until the ball is in the air, even if they are certain that the pass is going to be out to that section. There is very little chance of the opponent making any sizable gain on a flat pass, and thus we would rather have our halfbacks be sure that no long passes can be thrown. A good halfback can always come up fast enough to tackle the man in the flat soon after he catches a pass. The halfbacks should never take their eyes off the ball. As soon as it leaves the quarterback's hands every pass defender should "fly" toward it. No matter how far away from the individual the ball may be, we want every man to get over to it just as fast as he possibly can.

LATERAL PASSES

Laterals on the end of a pass have become extremely popular during the past few years and we have had to adopt a rule to guard against them. Whenever there is a possibility of a lateral being tossed to an outside man, we ask our halfbacks to take care of this man. This is extremely important, and even if there is no lateral, this maneuver forces the ball carrier in toward some of the defender's teammates. Such a play works either as a pass to the end which he in turn laterals to the halfback, or as a pass to one halfback in the flat followed by the other coming around on a type of delayed motion movement and taking the lateral. Both of these plays are contained in our offense, and consequently we drill our defense against them often.

INTERCEPTIONS

We require every man on defense to head in the direction the ball is thrown the minute it leaves the passer's hand. This means the linemen as well as the backs. If the pass is completed, we want them to be there in order to make the tackle. If it is intercepted we want them to be there to act as blockers. One rule that we have set down in regard to interception will prove very valuable to any coach who has not started to use it. Have a set rule that the first man over to the ball after an interception shall block the intended receiver. Ever so many times our backs have made exceptional catches of enemy passes only to be brought down before they could take five steps. We studied our movies for quite some time before we noticed that in nine out of ten cases the tackle was being made by the intended receiver. Now, as soon as one of our men intercepts a pass, we ask the teammate nearest him to block back on the enemy for whom the pass was intended. If there happen to be two of our men in the area at the time of interception, we ask them immediately to voice who is going to take care of the enemy.

SPECIFIC ASSIGNMENTS

We mentioned before that all halfbacks should employ the following philosophy when playing defense; that is, "It's going to be a pass," until you are absolutely positive that it will be a running play. The men always come up fast on a running play, but they very seldom can catch a receiver after he once gets behind them. Watch the opponents continually as the play is formulating. Many tips are given away by enemy players if only the defense will be on the lookout for them.

The defensive backfield will line up according to what the situation is. Every man must know what down it is, how much time is remaining, and how far the enemy need go to reach the goal line. Next, the defensive men will keep their eyes on the offensive ends. These are the men that will lead the defenders to the ball on a pass play. If each back will watch the end on his side, and the wingback in a single wing, he will be able to diagnose the play much faster. If the flanker stops and actually blocks the opposing linemen, then it is safe to assume that it is going to be a running play. When the end "flies" out, or brush blocks your teammate, it is time to be on your toes for a forward pass. While waiting for the ball to be snapped, the backs will eye the ends; meanwhile their split vision keeps the movements of the backfield under surveillance.

The *halfbacks* should turn everything inside; that is, whenever a potential pass receiver comes downfield, the halfback should endeavor to make this man run inside of him. In this manner, if the man does catch the ball, he will be heading in the direction of our safety man. The defenders must never allow anyone to get behind them, nor should they get too close to the receiver. The *safety man* must be conservative, since he is our last hope. We want him to move in fast when he is absolutely certain where the ball is going. Many times if the halfback is staying behind the receiver the safety man can gamble on cutting in front to intercept the ball. This should never be done unless the safety is positive that his teammate is behind.

We advocate vocal signals in our pass defensive set-up. Whenever one of our men spots a pass formulating, we want him to inform his teammates. For instance, if an end comes into one territory and then cuts fast into the adjoining area, we like our halfbacks to shout "end across." The halfback should move with this man until he definitely leaves the territory, and he should be constantly on the lookout for a cut-

back. Meanwhile, he should be prepared to pick up any man crossing from the opposite side into his defensive zone. As soon as someone comes into his territory he is relieved of the responsibility of the first end who was crossing and assumes the liability of the new man entering his area.

If two potential receivers come downfield at the same time, the halfback is directly responsible for the man on the outside. Naturally we like to see our men take care of their entire zone, but if the opponent is trying to disconcert the defender, we ask our back to stay with the man on the outside. Should the enemy pass to the inside man, the safety man can come up fast before too much damage has been done. If both of these men turn in, our back should be on the alert for the opposite end coming across. Many teams use this criss-cross maneuver in an attempt to unnerve the defender.

LINEMEN ON PASS DEFENSE

Linemen should be quick to learn that a pass is coming up from the type of block that the opponents are attempting to accomplish. The majority of teams use the stand-up method of pass blocking; that is, the linemen come up fast and raise their elbows high in order to shield the passer and be able to retreat with the onrushing linemen. As soon as they see this the men up front should inform their teammates that a pass is coming up, and then they should go about trying to bat it down.

The *ends* should attempt to crash fast and rush the passer. The more aggressive they are on this play, the more inaccurate the passer will be. We are not in favor of roughing the passer because the real good competitors will not slow down no matter how rough it gets. We ask our ends to crash in quickly and attempt to tackle the man high so he cannot get the ball away. We have seen many great passers complete aerials after having been hit with a solid leg tackle. If both ends will come in fast and tall, it will narrow down the passing

lane and the quarterback will have to move hurriedly. One of the most pleasant surprises we have ever received during a football contest came in our Purdue game of 1946 when Leon Hart and Bob Skoglund, our two ends, were rushing the Purdue passer. Leon hit him fairly hard with a shoulder tackle, and the ball bounced high in the air; Bob Skoglund was about one step away, and he caught the ball and ran for a touchdown. Such "breaks" as these are what we strive for when we tell our players that they must keep their heads up for sixty minutes.

The *tackles* will find it a little tougher to get in fast enough to block the pass; however, by varying their tactics they should be able to fake the enemy out of position and slide into the secondary. Their man will strive to make them run to the outside, so a double head fake may be necessary—first in, then out—before they can get through the middle.

Generally when it is a pass situation we have but one *guard* in the line. We have always used the *right guard* as the linebacker and kept our *left guard* in the forward wall.

One trick that coaches must guard against on pass defense is the screen pass. Overaggressive linemen are likely to be in the enemy backfield before they realize that is just where the opponent wants them. Experience is the best teacher here, but let your players get it on the practice field. The men should be cautious enough so that they will know immediately when the opposing lineman is purposely letting them through. If the defenders get through before they realize the "screen" is on, they should come up just as tall as they possibly can and attempt to bat down the ball. Such a pass must of necessity be thrown low, and a tall lineman may be in a position to knock it off its course.

Our last words to a pass defensive unit are that they must never take their eyes off the ball. If it is impossible for them to knock it down, they should be on the move as potential tacklers, and if it is intercepted, their task is to look for someone to block.

19

Pre-Game Warmup

THE PRACTICE SESSION that we plan for just prior to the game is one of the most important of our entire season. It is at this time that your lads become accustomed to the crowded stadium. It is then that they have an opportunity to work out the "jitters" that come to even the best athletes in the world. They have had a full night's sleep, and from the time they arise in the morning until they arrive at the locker room the general topic of conversation on campus is the forthcoming game. Unless you give them a good strong workout, you will notice that they are too tense when the opening whistle blows. True, once the game is under way they will shake off this tenseness, but a good team may have registered six points before this happens.

We have formulated a definite plan in regard to a pre-game warmup, and we like to think that it is just about what the doctor ordered. The field is divided in two lengthwise, and we take an entire end zone and one-half of the playing area; that is, one entire side, which allows our kickers to kick the length of the field if possible. The opponent has the opposite end zone and the adjoining side of the field. The warmup drill should take exactly twenty minutes, and these twenty minutes are of vital importance to every single member of your squad. Have your specialists work particularly hard at this time, since they will be sent into the game on split second notice and should have a good limbering up exercise before the game starts.

EXERCISE

Our Captain leads the entire team onto the field in a trot. All the men assemble in the end zone that has been assigned to them, where we have one of our assistant coaches lead them in calisthenics. First, we give them the seat roll, which loosens up all of the muscles of the body, and secondly, we have them all work on the hurdler's spread. These two exercises, which we use every day in practice, are the two best that we know for completely relaxing the lads prior to an important contest.

Next, we have the boys run a few wind sprints, still under the direction of the assistant coach. They assume their offensive stance, and on the signal from the coach they sprint out for four or five very fast steps. Do this until you notice that the men are doing it in unison and that all of your squad members seem to be ready to move. You may notice that it will take longer before some games than it will for others. This is not a conditioning exercise at this time, but rather a little workout to help the boys with their timing before the game commences.

TEAM FORMATIONS

Team formations come next. We plan to dress four full teams for our home games and three complete teams for the games away from home. In addition to this, we usually have a few extra defensive men, and possibly a kicker or two. Have them line up in teams, each with a ball. Start two from each end of the field and have them run a few plays up and down the field until the quarterback and his ball carriers have hit their perfect timing stride. This too will vary with

the importance of the contest. Do not rush them—let their actions tell you when they have had enough of this. The teams will then retire to specified spots on the gridiron. Spread the four teams out so that you will have the maximum amount of room for passing.

Pass Patterns.—We generally have one team line up at each goal line, and the other two line up back to back at the fifty-yard stripe. From these positions they must run through every pass play in the book. This means at least one pass to each eligible receiver. Make sure that every man has an opportunity to catch a pass. Have your quarterback work especially hard on your short spot passes. You should have your receivers geared up so that they can hit the spot exactly when the ball arrives. This has all been perfected in practice, but if they do not try it once in the stadium on the day of the game, they will not have the necessary confidence in themselves. It is merely a routine gesture, but you will be absolutely amazed at how relaxed your pass catchers will appear after they have drawn the pigskin into their arms. Make certain if one of your men drops the ball that he is given a second, and even a third, opportunity to catch a pass. All these little psychological points are of utmost importance. They help to get the "butterflies" out of the stomachs of the players.

While running these pass patterns we have the few extra men who are dressed assume defensive positions. The fact that these men are stationed in the pass zone makes the receiver a little more alert than he would ordinarily be if the field were clear. What we do is have our center line up over the ball, with the quarterback in his usual position behind him. The ends then line up in their customary positions, with all eligible receivers directly behind them. By using two balls, we have our passer throwing almost all the time he is out there. The fact that we have at least five eligible receivers in each group makes it possible for one man to be running all the time.   Always have your men hustling during this session, since it creates a favorable impression on everybody in the stands.

Punting.—While the teams are still lined up in this position we have them practice their punting.   At Notre Dame our quarterbacks have always done our kicking; therefore we have our remaining backs go down to the opposite end to receive the kicks.   The teams line up in regular offensive formation and follow through on their individual assignments as soon as the ball is snapped.   We want all of our linemen to speed downfield and be in a position to halt the man returning the kick.   The ball carrier should run hard with the ball right up until he is definitely hemmed in by the potential tacklers.   We do not want any tackling done in this pre-game warmup, but we do ask the men to carry out every movement right up until they would start to make the tackle. Have your kickers pick out a certain spot on the gridiron and aim their punts at that space.   We firmly believe that an accurate punter is a much more valuable asset to a team than a man who can kick the ball farther without knowing exactly where it is going to fall.   This ability means a great deal today because the majority of teams have punt return specialists whom they use for nothing but bringing back kicks.   These men are extremely tricky, and unless they have to chase the ball, you may find that they are returning it the entire distance.

Place Kicking.—We then have our "point-after" men adjourn to our end of the field and spend a few moments kicking the ball through the uprights.   This is a phase of football that depends a great deal on timing and coördination.   We ask the man to work at it until he has kicked about five in a row through the goal posts, and then we feel that he has found the proper range.   While he is doing this we have our kickoff man working on his specialty.   We use two types of kickoffs at Notre Dame, and as yet I am not absolutely certain which one I prefer. First, we use the conventional up-right, end-over-end kickoff. We have also had an amazing amount of success with the flat kickoff. That is, we just lay the ball on its side on the ground and have our man kick right into the center of the ball. This sends it careening crazily down the field, and makes it exceptionally difficult for the enemy to handle. If you can find a kicker such as Lou Groza, of the Cleveland Browns, who is capable of kicking the ball beyond the playing field every time, then there is no doubt that the conventional upright kickoff is best. However, in college and high school football you will seldom find a lad who has the power to kick a ball that far consistently. That is why we often use the other method. Notre Dame has been extremely fortunate in recovering many fumbles on the kickoff in the past few years, and we are firmly convinced that the principal reason our opponents have lost possession of the ball is because they cannot judge its next movement as it bounds down toward them. One of our biggest breaks of the 1947 season came when Southern California fumbled the opening kickoff. The ball was recovered by our Captain, George Connor, and Notre Dame went on from that spot to initiate the scoring for that afternoon.

THE DRESSING ROOM

When we see that the kickoff men have loosened up their leg muscles, we sound the "All up" call. As soon as this is heard all of our boys sprint over toward the bench and gather in a large circle. From there the captain leads them back into the dressing room at a fairly fast dog trot. They should have returned to the dressing room approximately ten to fifteen minutes before game time. This gives them a few minutes to relax and gives the coaching staff an opportunity to outline any last minute strategy. With the pre-game warmup complete, you will find that we have done absolutely everything that we will be called upon to do in the game except make the actual tackles.   Without attempting to appear egotistical, we would like to say that we are firmly convinced that this little loosening up plan of ours is a wonderful thing for the team.   You can readily notice the difference in the men's emotions before and after they start this brief session.

When the men gather in the dressing room prior to the contest we review briefly the plan of attack we would like to have them follow during the afternoon.   We do not like to restrict our quarterbacks, but we do explain our general impression of what they will most likely face, and if such is the case, we tell them how we desire to have them combat the enemy plans.   This is a most important psychological time, and coaches must be exceptionally careful not to appear too optimistic.   Neither can they afford to show too much pessimism.   If optimism is prevalent in your pre-game talk, the lads may become overconfident.   However, if you go too far in the opposite direction, you may notice that your lads are beginning to wonder if they are capable of defeating the opponent.   If they are facing a very tough opponent, we like to tell our men that it is our sincere belief that the teams are about equally matched and we feel that if they will get out there and hustle for sixty minutes and battle for every inch of ground, they will emerge the victors.   Impress upon your boys that you have implicit faith in them and their ability to get things done.

GAME DUTIES FOR COACHES

We have set up a plan for our coaching staff that we believe is very important in regard to the outcome of the game.   As a general rule we have two, and sometimes three, assistant coaches with us on the day of a game.   The remaining members of our staff and the freshman coaches are usually assigned to scouting tasks.

ASSISTANT COACH

One member of our staff always sits on the bench with us. He has many very important jobs to fulfill. First, he must keep accurate account of the number of time outs we take in each period. One of his biggest jobs is to have his substitutes all lined up and ready to enter the game. We ask him to check the starting lineup as soon as the whistle blows to start the game. As he looks over the eleven men on the field, he should list the men who will be the number one replacements for those boys in action. Assuming that things operate smoothly, we like to substitute an entire team at the start of the second quarter. This gives our first team a chance to rest and think over the situation. In this case the assistant coach will line up the second eleven in the closing minutes of the first period. He then gives them any instructions that we may have discussed while the initial quarter was under way. He should have a notebook with him at all times to write down every suggestion that the head coach mentions. When "briefing" the replacements he should refer to his notes and inform them of anything that might make their tasks easier.

Should an injury occur during the opening period all the assistant need do is check his second team group and call the man for that position. When such an unfortunate circumstance occurs he should immediately substitute the name of the third team player in the vacancy. While the second team is performing on the field he should have two lineups ready to substitute on split-second notice. One is, of course, the starting team, and the other would be the third team. If we were fortunate enough to build a sizable lead early in the game, it would be prudent on our part to inject the third team into the lineup in order to learn how they operate under pressure. All of these things the assistant on the bench must do in an organized fashion. If he is completely confident as to what he is doing, you will find that such a spirit will permeate the men he is substituting.

Another all-important duty of the man on the bench is to be on our end of the phone that connects with the top of the press box. Here we have our other assistant located. If possible, it is best to have a backfield man and a lineman in the booth. These men are watching every play, and as soon as they spot a weakness in the enemy defense they inform us over the phone. The assistant makes notes on all of their suggestions and evaluates them immediately. Some of the information should be brought to the head coach's attention at once, whereas there are other points that should be passed along to the team that will be going into the game in a few minutes. If, for instance, our backfield coach in the booth tells us that the defense looks extremely vulnerable to a "29H pass," we would have the assistant relay such information to our second string quarterback. It is most pleasing to have received information from the booth that a certain play will work well, and then to have this play called by our quarterback before we have an opportunity to send in a substitute signal caller. When this occurs frequently, you can feel sure that the young man over the center is fast developing into a "T Master."

THE BENCH

Our policy in regard to the bench situation has always been to have five or six small chairs out in front of the regular bench. In the group in front we like to have the head coach, the assistant coach, the reserve quarterbacks, and the student manager. The reasons for the inclusion of coaches and quarterbacks is quite obvious, while we believe that the student manager is one of the more important cogs in a collegiate football machine. During the course of a game we have many occasions to call on the student manager to take care of important details for us. We usually like to have our quarterback and whoever is most likely to be substituted sitting next to the head coach. This gives us an opportunity to bring to their attention any little weaknesses that we may spot in the enemy defense. The remainder of the squad should pair up according to positions on the full length bench that runs along the sideline behind the chairs. We ask them to sit according to positions in order that the men in each group will have a natural tendency to watch those who are performing at their respective positions and to discuss the comparative strength and weak points of the opposing team. Impress upon your lads that they must think nothing but football for the entire afternoon, whether they be on the bench or in the game. In comparison with what they have been willing to put out all week, it is little to ask that they concentrate diligently on the main event of the afternoon.

The thought we would like to leave with our readers in regard to the pre-game period is that the coach should do his best to make sure the boys are occupied, both physically and mentally, for as much of the time as possible from noon right up until the kickoff. When one of our boys is asked if he was nervous before a big game, we like to hear him say, "I didn't have time to think of getting nervous."

20

How to Watch a Football Game

TO THE FOOTBALL FANS of America we of the coaching profession owe a tremendous debt of gratitude. It is these loyal fans who have made it possible for football to be put on a paying basis, thus allowing the sport to become one to which a man can devote his entire time and make a living. True, no one will ever become rich coaching football, but it is a profession that has risen to a point where it now commands considerable respect in the community.

In view of the fact that we have spent almost all of our life coaching football, we should like to pass on to the fans some information that we believe will help them to enjoy the games a bit more. Whenever we attend a football game as a spectator, we make it a point to arrive at the stadium at least thirty minutes before game time. In addition to avoiding the big pre-game traffic jams, we are thereby afforded a chance to look over both teams as they are going through their pre-game warmups. As soon as a man gets to the field he should purchase a program and open it to the players' roster.

BEFORE THE KICKOFF

The first thing to do while the boys are warming up is to pick out the starting teams with the aid of your program. When you have the numbers fixed in your mind begin to concentrate on the players' stature and any hints that will help you to recognize them when it is impossible to determine what their number is.   Make a special study of the backs. When watching a "T" team you do not have to worry about the quarterback because he is always over the center.   However, pick out some outstanding characteristic in each running back and make a mental note of it.   Once you feel that you are fairly familiar with the first team, move on into the second team backfield.   If you have the time, study the linemen also, but you will find that generally the linemen will stay close to their positions.   Thus, if you are familiar with their numbers, you will not have too much trouble identifying them.

The teams will go through individual maneuvers, at which time it is good to notice who is throwing the passes and who is doing the kicking.   If you happen to see a halfback on a "T" team who is passing fairly well, catalogue this information; during the game he may surprise everyone in the stands by throwing a pass.   Check the numbers of the men who are doing the punting in practice.   See if they are all quarterbacks, and if not, find out what position they do play.   Many teams have their linemen doing the kicking, and then again you may find a fullback who is capable of getting off a very good quick kick.

Study the pass receivers.   Later you will get a great deal of enjoyment from seeing a pass completed to a man whom you picked out in the practice period as the outstanding pass receiver.   Notice how these boys catch the ball and what kind of pass they seem to receive better than others.   Be on the sharp lookout for a third or fourth string back who seems to have exceptional pass catching ability.   Late in the game you may see this boy being substituted, and then it will please you to follow his actions as a "prayer" pass is being thrown to him.   This is something that happens quite frequently in a football game.   When the boys leave the field notice how much speed and hustle they have.   If, in your opinion, the teams are about equal in ability, it may well be the team that sprints on and off the field that wins the ball game. We always ask our Captain to lead the team on the field, both to the practice sessions and prior to the start of the game. This gentleman will trot all the way from the locker room right up to the bench.

THE KICKOFF

As soon as the teams line up for the kickoff you should run down your lineup and check to be sure that all of the boys are in there. When the ball is in the air watch the movements of the linemen on the side of the field to which the ball is headed, and observe how quickly the offside linemen get across into blocking position. Many fans are not aware that hours are spent on trying to develop the perfect kickoff return. The best backs will take advantage of every block that is thrown by their teammates. One of our happiest memories is Terry Brennan's return of the Army kickoff in 1947. There was never a hand laid on Terry, and this was due mainly to two things. Primarily, Terry is a great runner, not the trickiest nor the fastest back we have ever coached, but one who makes use of every teammate he has on the field. Secondly, the blocking by his fellow players was excellent. The combination of these two elements made it possible for this Milwaukee youngster to carry the ball ninety-seven yards to a touchdown on the opening play of our "hump" game that year. Every one of our linemen followed through on his assignment as if the very outcome of the game depended on that one play, and we feel that possibly it did.

PLAYS FROM SCRIMMAGE

Once the game has settled down to plays that run from the line of scrimmage, we must concentrate intently on the maneuvers made by the "T" quarterback. If the fans will just glance over the basic plays we have given in the earlier part of the book before going to a game, they will be amazed to find that they can analyze almost every play as similar to one of those diagrammed. Watch the quarterback for the first few plays until you have become accustomed to his method of operation. Once you have his qualities catalogued, you will find it much easier to follow the ball. Look at his feet and find out whether he is making a reverse pivot or not. After observing him closely for a few plays, you will find that it is possible to visualize what he is intending to do before he completes his pivot. As for instance, if his left foot is forward and he starts a reverse pivot, then you should look directly toward the halfbacks. Usually the one who is not going to receive the ball has made some preliminary movement that takes him out of the play, thus leaving you one man to follow. As this man comes in to get the ball watch his movements very closely. From up in the stands it is much easier to tell whether he is trying to fake or not. If he flashes past the quarterback and doubles way over then you had best look back to the signal caller and see if he does not still have the ball.

Try to analyze the situation and think what you would call if you were the field general under the same conditions. If it is a large yardage situation and they are in a position where a pass might prove of great help, observe the quarterback very closely. See what he calls, and try to decide why an "11 pass" would work better than a "43 pass." If it is a small yardage situation on second or third down, look for the quick-opener. On such a play keep your eye on the most dependable back, not the most spectacular. Many times you will notice that your tricky backs are not too potent when called upon to pick up a yard or two. Their specialty is zigging and zagging for about thirty yards; therefore, when there is a scatback in at one halfback position, the only ones you have to watch are the fullback and the other halfback.

As a rule, the man with the best yardage percentage will be called upon under such circumstances.

As the game progresses and you find it fairly easy to follow the progress of the ball, begin to watch the linemen. I honestly believe that once a fan sees how each lineman operates on certain plays, he will enjoy the game much more. Concentrate on the guards a great deal, because whenever you see a guard pull he will lead you to the ball carrier. On a play such as our end around, both guards pull and make a very interesting picture for one who loves good, hard, clean football.

WATCHING THE DEFENSE

Naturally the majority of fans go into the stadium rooting for their favorite team. Therefore, we like to give a few hints on how to watch your home team when they are on defense. They will give you innumerable tips on what type of play is expected. As mentioned, we have three basic types of defenses—the six-, the five-, and the seven-man line. We vary these as much as possible, and once in a great while we will try a four if the opponent has an exceptionally potent pass offense. Notice that the defensive men are always on the move. They never want the opponent to know exactly what the defense is. Keep a close watch on the linebackers. Whenever you see them jump into the line, then you can expect a powerful running play. The center is the defensive quarterback of most every team. You will see him with his back to the opponent while they are in the huddle. He will be giving the defensive signals to his teammates. He gives these on the assumption that the enemy will most likely follow the usual manner of play. If it is a small yardage situation, he might signal for a seven-man line. The ends make an interesting study as they continually vary their defensive tactics. Most interesting it is to watch an end throw his body in the way of the interference on an end sweep.

If the fans will remember such things as when a play is most likely to work, they will derive a great deal of enjoyment from trying to second guess the quarterback. We like to think that the quick opener or one of its variations is best for first down. Our quarterbacks temper this with an occasional forward pass to initiate the play. Many times this catches the opponents completely off guard. If the offense is doing rather well through the line, they should throw very few forward passes. Second down is usually the best time to throw a pass. If it works, you have the long gain; if not, you still have one more down before being forced to kick. We do not like to see our boys pass too often on third down because it is too much of a gamble. As a rule, all teams will punt on fourth down unless they have less than two yards to go for the first down. We saw Sid Luckman of the Chicago Bears pull a very smart trick one Sunday afternoon. It was the Bears' ball, fourth and one. When they came out of the huddle Luckman hurried up with the center, and on "Hike" he had the ball and had made the first down before the opponents were ready to start the play. This is the type of football that pleases the fans, and they look for it hopefully.

OTHER AIDS TO ENJOYMENT

We firmly believe that if the majority of fans in the country will just study the program for a short time before each game and make themselves fully acquainted with all of the players, they will get even more enjoyment out of the football games during the fall. The pre-game newspaper reports should bring every loyal fan into the stadium with plenty of information as to the relative ability of the two teams and the individual characteristics of most of the players. When we go out on the field and see a stadium filled with people, we always hope that each and every person in the stands is getting as much enjoyment out of watching our lads perform as we ourselves do.   Football is a great American game, which has been made extremely popular by the generosity of the thousands of fans all over the country, and we should like to take this opportunity to express our heartfelt gratitude to these football-loving people who have made it possible for us to work in such an enjoyable profession.

A book on football would scarcely be complete if we were to omit mention of that great personage who is the medium between the football field and the millions of fans who cannot attend the games on Saturday.   Yes, we are speaking of the sports writers.   These gentlemen, who have befriended us many times, do more for football in America than all of the people who are more closely affiliated with the sport.   We believe that football could be carried on in this country without their aid, but it would have about as much appeal to the public as does outdoor swimming at the North Pole. It is my sincere wish that I could list here the names of the press men who have been so very kind to me since I first became acquainted with the game of football.   I am privileged to be able to say that I have among some of my closest friends sports writers from almost every section of the country. Wherever we have gone we have always been treated royally by the gentlemen of the press, and I should like to thank each and every one of them publicly for all that they are doing toward making football one of the top sports in America.

21

The Value of Football

WE SHOULD LIKE very much to bring this book to a close by spending a few minutes estimating what we believe an American boy gets out of the game of football. Many people are wont to say that these lads get nothing more than a number of bumps and bruises. It is very true that the players receive more than their share of hard knocks during their playing careers, but I should like to know of any walk of life in which men are not called upon to face setbacks. We realize that these setbacks are not always of a physical nature, but we believe if a young man learns at an early age that it is imperative for him to come back and work harder than ever after he receives a tough blow, he will have the makings of a successful American citizen. There has never been a road to success that was strewn with roses, and we want our young men to learn while young that they have to make their way through the thorns.

We all know that we live in the world's greatest democracy, but how often do we stop to think why America stands head and shoulders above every other nation in the world. Is it because of the fruits of our large-scale productive efforts? We are inclined to think not. We think that the fact that the United States has never lost a battle is the main reason why she is the most respected country in this troubled world. Certainly there are some nations that would like very much to take over our unparalleled sources of supplies, but why is it that they do not? Many have tried. Yet because of something known throughout the world as the "American Spirit,"

229

the Stars and Stripes have never taken second place on any battlefield. With this in mind, we ask you to think back and ask yourself where our young men developed the qualities that go to make up a good fighting man. Where did they learn loyalty? Where did they acquire the burning desire to stay in there and fight until ultimate victory was achieved? These traits are something that cannot be found in textbooks, nor can they be learned in the lecture room. It is on the athletic fields that our boys acquire these winning ways that are as much a part of the American life as are freedom of speech and of the press. It is my sincere hope that none of my five children will ever be called upon to face another war, and I certainly am not in favor of having them in a continual state of frenzied preparedness as were German youth in World War II. However, it is my most fervent desire to be able to have the feeling that whenever my sons are required to enter any type of competitive activity, they will go out and strive diligently to win. *The American way is the winning way.*

In most communities the first fourteen years of the average boy's life are planned and protected by the Boy Scouts and similar organizations. When the lad grows up and reaches the age of twenty-one he is usually on his own and is prepared to take care of himself. What happens to the young man between the ages of fourteen and twenty-one? It is here that we find the "forgotten boy." Too often the boy of fourteen, fifteen, sixteen, and up to twenty is allowed to shift for himself. For young men of this age there are very few guiding hands to help them choose the correct path in life. One look at the daily newspapers will prove to you that the police records in all of our cities show a large number of young men falling into the early stages of crime—and not only is the number increasing, but the offenses are becoming much more serious.

What are we going to do about this situation? Making speeches and writing books alone will not be the cure. Resolutions and high sounding quotes from social workers' bulletins will not do the job. But the men who are in the coaching profession are the people who have the opportunity to mold the life of the youth of America. They are the ones who must carry the load if teen-age America is going to ripen into responsible manhood. Coaches, we can impart this knowledge by means of incentives and good example. Give the "forgotten boy" something to shoot at. Present to him a formula based on experience and the reward that comes from clean living, hard-hitting competition, and the spirit of sportsmanship. Inspire the youth with the exploits of his heroes—the Knute Rocknes, the Babe Ruths, the Lou Gehrigs, the Jack Dempseys, and any local heroes that your lads can look up to. All of the above mentioned men went through the same years of critical environment that our teen-age youngsters face today. When they came to the crossroads there was a helping hand and a guiding heart to influence them by example, by counsel, by opportunity, and by patient understanding. Some people have called the years between fourteen and twenty the "No Man's Land" of boyhood. The founding of a civic movement which makes every lad in a given community want to become part of the athletic program of that section will provide the right incentive. Good examples and environment will soon erase the blemish of delinquency and eliminate the problem of the "forgotten boy."

During the time that I was in the service with the U. S. Navy I developed a new appreciation of being an American. I was privileged to see our fighting men in combat and to be with them on the lonely islands of the Pacific. Here I saw the youth of yesterday as the greatest fighting machine ever assembled in the history of the world.

When I returned to Notre Dame, and our football squad reported for spring practice in 1946, I relived my experience in the Pacific because on the field before me were real American boys—a carbon copy of democracy. Every boy had an equal chance; his religion or nationality played no part in his making the football team. They all seemed to know that they were to compete on equal terms and that if they possessed the ability and spirit, they could make our ball club.

Those afternoons of preliminary practice were hard. The young men had to be responsive to discipline; they had to be willing to carry out assignments. They never lost sight of the fact that there must be an individual accomplishment and that some day they would put their skills together and represent their school as a team. *This is democracy* as I see it—just as in our submarines in the Pacific every boy had a part to play in the operation of his ship, and he accepted it as an opportunity to serve his country.

All of this leads me to the willingness of these men to practice hour after hour because they had an ideal, which was to become a member of the Notre Dame football squad. I think that this training is very important to the future of America because the boys were not dissatisfied nor did they complain or try to upset the coach's plans, which is significant when one observes the conduct of some people in our country today. On Saturday afternoons in the stadia where we appeared last fall there was always a thrill even greater than the football game, and that came when the band would march to the flagpole and while thousands stood with heads bared, our grand old flag was unfurled! Then the crowds would settle back to the business of the afternoon, where the skills and competitive spirit of these young American boys were pitted against each other in a wholesome contest that demanded the same alertness and courage and persistence that will be required of them when their college days are over and they step out into the business world. I also thought of the "Old Grads" of many schools sitting in the stands, whose minds were taken back by the scenes before them to their own school days, and I am quite sure that many of them found inspiration and a new determination to carry on just a little better in whatever work they were engaged.

These great crowds, many from distant places, again represented democracy in action. They had their favorite team and they rooted hard for it to win! They were not complaining or finding fault or trying to upset the game of football through undercover agitation. They were citizens who were there seeking an outlet for their competitive emotions. They were individuals—not regimented by anyone. If they did not like the game, they could leave at any time. *They were Americans,* and football is an American sport that develops Americans and keeps alive the things that America stands for.

There is no room for "isms" at a football game. I can think of no one more out of place at a football game than a proponent of one of these "isms." He would not understand the cheering thousands. He would consider it a waste of time. The enthusiasm of the players as well as the spectators would grate on his nerves. People of all classes, religions, and races being there together for the common purpose of enjoying themselves would make him very unhappy because it is his creed to sow seeds of discontent and dissatisfaction with what *we* have. As one subversive foreign agent reported to his leader, when asked why he was unable to overthrow the democratic way of life, "The trouble with that country is that there are too many Americans in it." All of the things that go together to make this country great must continually be defended from any attack. Youth movements do not strengthen a country, either militarily or athletically, as was conclusively proven by the smashing American victories in World War II and in London at the 1948 Olympics. We must always preserve the great sporting spirit of the American people. It is part of our nature to be competitive. Through this medium we have become the greatest nation in the world; we will continue to be so long as we preserve our rights, meet our problems as individuals, and avoid being fettered by regimentation and standardization of our abilities. The persons charged with the responsibility of our ship of state might well agree with him who wrote, "There is a peace more destructive of manhood, more destructive of the living man, than war is destructive to his material body. Chains are worse than bayonets."

While on the subject of Americanism and what our boys get out of football we should like to make a point about lads of foreign parentage who have represented many great institutions on the football field. Many people have poked fun at Notre Dame because of some of the unpronounceable names that have appeared in her lineups down through the years. However, we are extremely proud of all of these boys, and we feel that they are to be highly congratulated for the sacrifices they have made to receive their degrees. Several of these lads come from homes where English is not even spoken, and when they arrived in college they found that it was necessary for them to work much harder than other boys in order to grasp the subjects. Yet down through the years we have had very few boys of foreign descent fail out of school. Many boys get up early and spend all of their spare time with the books in order that they may become well-educated American citizens by the time they leave school. These lads are to be admired, and we shall always be happy to have boys with the long names on our football team, because in many cases the long name is synonymous with long hours of hard work and sacrifice, and for this there is *no substitute*.

On a successful football team a boy must learn to work for the good of the whole and to subordinate his personal interests to the good of the team. An individualist seldom, if ever, manages to achieve any lasting accomplishments. To illustrate this point, here at Notre Dame we refer to the Four

Horsemen and the Seven Mules of 1924, the 1929 and 1930 teams of Coach Rockne, as well as our own teams of 1941, 1943, 1946, 1947, and 1948, all of which really achieved greatness because they were composed of men who felt that if they did not produce 100 percent on every play the team would not be successful. It is the teams that are remembered more than the individuals.

Endurance is a quality that is essential to achievement. Physical endurance is tested often on the gridiron, and mental endurance is a direct result of hard work by a person to achieve his objective. We always tell our lads that when things appear especially rough they must remember that they are no easier for the opponent. Maybe he will be able to keep stride with them for fifty-nine minutes, but as a rule, if your men will keep working with the thought in mind that perhaps the opponent will weaken in the last minute of the game, then they will usually find that the competition is not quite so tough as they thought it was. The same holds true in the competitive battle of life.

A player's rise to fame is controlled only by his own willingness to reach such heights. We must never allow anyone to convince us that any other nation in the world enjoys this blessing as lavishly as we enjoy it here in America. We should never be persuaded to believe that these benefits just happened to "spring up" in our country. They have not sprung up in Japan, Germany, Russia, or China, and yet all of these lands are as rich, or richer, potentially than is our homeland. The American advantages have developed chiefly because we are blessed with the most successful form of government ever devised, and because in this great nation there are, proportionately speaking, more God fearing and God loving people than in any other section of the world.

It is our duty to defend the qualities that have made our country superior. Not long ago thousands of young Americans made the supreme sacrifice for the sake of a finer America and a better world. The least we can do is to vow solemnly that we will at all times strive diligently to make America the kind of nation that they wanted it to be, for all time to come.

Index

A

Abstention, 3
Accuracy in passing, 105
Aggressiveness, 3-4, 58
  blocking, 157, 186
  passing, 125
Alcoholic beverages, 3
Alibis, 9
All-America Conference, 144
All-American teams, 37
"All-up" call, 6, 217
"American spirit," 229-233
Analytical ability, 127
Angle pass, 107-108, 153
Army, 30, 32, 45, 70, 80, 92, 99, 141, 192, 203-204, 224
Ashbaugh, Russell, 151, 153, 192, 204
Assignments, 7, 18, 232
  coaches, 6-7
  pass defense, 209-211
  pass protection, 118-122
  positions, 150
  quick opener, 41-42
  understanding, 186
Assistant coaches, 6-7
  game duties, 219-220
Audiences, 130
  game-enjoyment aids, 227-228
  how to watch a game, 222-228
  pleasing the, 16, 57

B

Backs, 54-55
  defense, 151-153
  on pass defense, 207-208
  overworked, 130

Backs—*Continued*
  passes to, 110-112
  pass protection, 118
Ball carrying, 43, 134
  feeding, 138
  halfback and fullback, 146-154
Ball grasping, center, 178-179
"Ball hawks," 201
Ball passing, 102-117
  "riding," 136-137
Banana pass, 109-110
Basketball court drilling, 131
Behavior of players, 1-11
"Bellying," 49
Bench, the, 8, 220-221, 224
Bertelli, Angelo, 132, 143-145
"Between" pass, 109-110
Blackboard drills, 43
Blaik, Earl, 56
Blanchard, Doc, 203-204
Blocking, 14-15, 17, 21
  aggressiveness, 186
  center, by, 180-187
  downfield, 182-183
  end play, 155-161
  errors, 185-187
  good, 157
  halfback and fullback, 151
  offensive, 167
  pass essentials, 116, 124-126
  reverse shoulder block, 158-159
  stance, 156-157
Body block, 159
"Bread and butter" plays, 16, 22, 44, 130
Brennan, Terry, 15, 54, 92, 113, 192, 204-205, 224